Praise for

Must We Say We Did Not Love?

Throughout my 34 years as a clinical psychologist in private practice I have been aware of the need for closure rituals. Once clients have worked through loss, abuse, trauma, or life passages, they need to take the steps of integration, transcendence, and, finally, closure.

Many of my clients have expressed the wish to share rituals with a group of loved ones or friends at the end of their therapeutic work in order to have witnesses to this final step, to be surrounded by a circle of compassion.

I perceive the practice of closure rituals to be the last crucial step in the psychological healing process. Because of this, I am delighted that Dr. Naff is writing a book about such rituals. Due to her wide range and depth of knowledge in the fields of counseling, retreat and ritual facilitation, ministry, public speaking, university teaching, and creative writing, Dr. Naff is truly a gifted and brilliant expert. Mental health professionals will profit greatly from this resource.

Dr. Gisela Bergman, Clinical Psychologist, Eugene, OR

In a society that privatizes loss, leaving people ritually empty and ignorant of the power of symbolic acts, I am in desperate need of resources that offer compassionate hope and healing. Dr. Naff recognizes this chasm of grief and brings her sensitive spirit and brilliant mind to the task of providing words and actions that allow people to 'come full circle' in their lives filled with change. I am grateful for this upcoming resource and will recommend it highly to my colleagues.

Rev. Tiare L. Mathison-Bowie, Senior Pastor, First Presbyterian Church, Newton, IA

Through rich storytelling and clearly delineated principles, process guidelines and examples, Dr. Naff provides collaborative professionals and participants invaluable tools and sage guidance with which to facilitate the deep peace and lasting agreements that earmark the highest potential of collaborative practice.

Suzan Barrie Aiken, J.D., Collaborative Attorney and Mediator, President, Collaborative Family Law Professionals of Marin, Co-Chair, Collaborative Practice California, Third Annual State-Wide Conference

Dr. Monza Naff's *Must We Say We Did Not Love?* is a book I need in my lending library…yesterday!

Throughout the twentieth century and into the twenty-first science has been demonstrating again and again that we live in a continuous universe. But psychotherapy, running behind the times, has continued to stake its reputation on dated beliefs about a separate mind, a separate body, a separate person.

Dr. Naff recognizes at once the wounds caused by the illusion of separation, and she artfully creates rituals essential to the healing process—no-two-snowflakes-alike rituals which provide the sacred space to rediscover one's undisturbed wholeness.

Dr. Ann Jauregui, Co-founder of Marin Creek (Multidisciplinary Healing) Center, Berkeley, CA and Faculty, School of Clinical Psychology, John F. Kennedy University, Orinda, CA

In the collaborative practice community, we hold out the possibility that a couple can experience a dissolution process that is deeper, more profound and more meaningful than a mere settlement of their financial and parental rights. Dr. Naff invites us to offer our clients even more—sensitive, customized rituals to mark a life transition that can be more life-changing than those we traditionally have rituals for—births, marriages, and deaths. Dr. Naff's talent lies in creating a safe context that respects all the current feelings of each affected person. Whether the whole family participates, or each party creates their own separate ritual, each has the opportunity to honor the past, affirm the positive things that will continue, and set powerful intentions for the future. I believe that introducing our clients to the wisdom and mystery that ritual can offer will not only benefit them and their families, but will contribute to the healing and well-being of our greater community.

Nancy J. Foster, J.D., Exec. Director, Northern California Mediation Center, attorney, mediator, trainer and collaborative divorce attorney.

Must We Say We Did Not Love?

The Need
for Divorce Rituals
In Our Time

Monza Naff, Ph.D.

Wyatt-MacKenzie Publishing, Inc.

This book has grown out of a chapter on Divorce Rituals in Naff's forthcoming book, *To Brave the Pain of Spring: Non-Traditional Rituals for Times of Transition*.

Names and specific circumstances have been changed to protect the privacy of the participants in rituals described in this book. In some cases, elements of various similar rituals have been combined into one. In doing this I've tried to retain the spirit of individual rituals, making every effort to protect my clients and respect their wishes. I have, to the best of my ability, honored all legal and ethical standards in telling these stories, and I am deeply grateful for the advice I have been given on these matters. Any mistakes that remain are my own.

ISBN 978-1-932279-95-5

Library of Congress Control Number: 2008926043

Wyatt-MacKenzie Publishing, Inc.
DEADWOOD, OREGON

www.WyMacPublishing.com (541) 964-3314

Requests for permission or further information should be addressed to:
Wyatt-MacKenzie Publishing, 15115 Highway 36, Deadwood, Oregon 97430

This work is dedicated to my sister,

Debra Naff Dacus, MT-BC,

not because she will ever need it, but because she and I, together and individually, healed ourselves when our divorcing parents did not have a book like this, did not draw upon resources to make their divorce less painful, more bearable for their children.

I cannot imagine my life without you, Dub.

Nor do I want to.

Table of Contents

Prologue *Why I Am So Committed to Divorce Rituals—*
A Personal Story 1

Note to Divorcing Individuals or Couples without Children ... 7

Introduction *Must We Say We Did Not Love?* 9

CHAPTER 1: Amicable Divorce—A Ritual When a Couple
Has Children 25
    Guidelines 39

CHAPTER 2: Hostile Divorce—Each Parent Has Separate
Ritual with Children 43
    Guidelines 56

CHAPTER 3: Hostile Divorce: Parents Meet With Therapist
and Attorneys to Make Basic Commitments in Front of
Children 59
    Guidelines 67

CHAPTER 4: Abusive, Alcoholic Parent and Passive Parent:
A Ritual with Support Group and Discussion with Sons 71
    Guidelines–1 81
    Guidelines–2 89

CHAPTER 5: A Step-Parent Creates a Ritual for a
Teen-age Son 91
    Guidelines 98

CHAPTER 6: Divorcing Couple with Adopted Children
Ritualize Their Commitment to Continue Co-Parenting 101
    Guidelines 109

CHAPTER 7: Hostile Divorce—A Ritual for a Parent and Children After the Other Parent Has Left While the Children Are Away 111
  Guidelines 123

CHAPTER 8: Divorce in Which One Parent Completely Abandons Their Children—Ritual for Young Children 125
  Guidelines 136

CHAPTER 9: Divorcing Parent and Step-Parent Send Letter with Key Qualities of a Ritual to College-Age Children 139
  Guidelines–1 155
  Guidelines–2 156

CHAPTER 10: Divorcing Parents with Serious Religious Differences Find Mutually Respectful Agreement 157
  Guidelines 172

CHAPTER 11: One Parent in Divorcing Couple with Serious Power Differential Clarifies Her Values 173
  Guidelines 182

CHAPTER 12: Teens in Blended Family Create Ritual After Parents Separate and Take Their 'Own' Children, With No Visitation Planned 185
  Guidelines 194

Conclusion 195

Planning Guide 197

Acknowledgments 204

About the Author 206

Prologue

Why I Am So Committed to Divorce Rituals—
A Personal Story

I left home one morning at 8 a.m., told my mother, who was vacuuming, goodbye on the run, and when I came home at noon, found a note on the kitchen table: "I've gone to think things out. Mama." Her clothes were all gone from her closet.

I called my dad at work; he came home. We searched through the house for clues, but found only the house empty of my mother's belongings. My dad sat stunned at the kitchen table, looking at the note over and over. I sat in Mama's closet, smelling the faint scent of her perfume.

Soon it was time to pick up my sister, who was barely 13, from junior high, so I went to get her, to tell her Mama was gone. I called the dorm director late that afternoon, at the university where I was a sophomore, to say that I wouldn't be moving in—I'd be staying at home to take care of my dad and sister—my mom had left suddenly. She said,

"Thanks for letting me know."

That evening I also called my major professor, the woman I now call "my matron saint," told her I would be living at home instead of on campus so that we'd need to work out another pick-up place for papers I'd be grading for her. She showed up an hour later with a box full of paperback mystery novels. As she got back in her car to leave, she said, "I figured you would have need for escape, my dear."

Days and weeks went on, we had no idea where my mother was. She made no contact with my dad or with us kids. Friends (our friends, my mother's friends, dad's friends, family friends) called, came by, as shocked as we were. Some people dropped off food, as they would for a funeral. A few of my father's colleagues invited us over for dinner; conversations were stilted.

There were no calls to or from my mother's extended family (who knew where she was), none to or from my father's family either. After almost a month, Mama wrote a short note to my sister and me, told us she was in Las Vegas and that she was going to divorce Dad. She didn't ask how we were doing, or give a return address or a phone number. She asked us to try to understand.

It was on Thanksgiving Day that the divorce papers were served. Right in the middle of dinner, the doorbell rang, and when my dad answered it, there stood the sheriff. He handed Dad the papers, who took one look at them, threw them down on the entry table, shut the door on the sheriff, and walked down the hall to his bedroom.

Everyone at the table was frozen: I got up, looked at the papers in the blue envelope, walked down the hall to his room and then didn't open the door because I heard him weeping. I went back to my sister and our guests, sat back down in my place, and reported, "Divorce Papers."

I can't tell you much of what happened after that, but I have retained a few images: my grandmother going down the hall to talk to her son, my sister and I clearing the table, doing the dishes, and making small talk with the others. Eventually everyone except my grandparents left. My father never came out of his bedroom.

Of that Thanksgiving Day 1967, I don't remember if my sister Debbie and I looked at those papers again, talked with each other about our shattered lives, or wept. I don't know if we asked aloud why Dad didn't come out of his agony long enough to check on how the two of us were doing. I don't know if our grandparents offered any comfort, or if that was the moment they began acting as if my mother had never existed. I just know that I hated Thanksgiving for 25 years after that, and could never figure out why.

The divorce became final. Although we never discussed it, I believe my father felt broken, probably embarrassed, humiliated and angry. He was incompetent to run a household. He did not know how to cook, run a washing machine or dryer, iron his own shirts or handkerchiefs. I taught him.

But mostly I took care of all housekeeping chores since he worked all day every weekday and sometimes on weekends at the university where he was a professor at the seminary. And I was still a college student at that same university, carrying 21 hours a term in course work and working three work-study jobs.

We two girls, who had been abandoned, were left to ourselves to try to keep some semblance of normalcy in our lives, to heal individually and together from this sudden-as-a-stroke death of family as we had known it all our lives.

Looking back, 40 years later, I am still shocked to realize that while family members and old friends called off and on, beyond the generic "How are you holding up?" there was never any talk of how tenable this situation was for either of us daughters—the 19-year-old or the 13-year-old. No one ever asked if I needed help, if I wanted to consider how Dad and Debbie might get along if I returned to the dorm to continue my college years with some modicum of freedom. While it's still true that I would never have left my sister at that time, or my father to try to care for her alone, the issue is this: there was no conversation about it. What I can tell you is that no adult from our entire community of family or friends ever called, came over, asked us to come to their home, or took us somewhere beautiful in nature with the expressed intention of giving us a chance to talk freely and openly about what we were going through.

I do need to say that the two professors who knew me

best certainly asked me periodically, "How are you doing, Monza?" but I'm quite sure I most always answered, "OK, thanks for asking." And I also need to say, those mysteries my major professor brought me that first night served me well; hers was a profound kindness, the most practical I can remember from that year.

Life *did* go on. Debbie and I played games on some evenings, as we always had. We went to the movies, took camping trips and road excursions, we had parties. Sometimes Dad joined us. We had friends over for dinner.

I finished college and went on to graduate school. Dad and Mama both got re-married. Debbie graduated from high school and college and went out on her own. My sister and I are profoundly bonded, like war veterans. She tells me now that I'm more like her mother than Mama ever was after she was 13.

Both my sister and I are in long-term committed relationships. We love our work and are grateful for the happiness in our lives. We've come through that ancient, soul-shaking storm.

I wish there had been a book like this that *someone* might have handed to my father. Or to the therapist that Dad, Debbie, and I finally consulted. Or to our pastor. Or to one of our teachers or friends. I know it would have been deeply useful as a guide for knowing how to talk about the divorce and how to ritualize our loss and hopes, our regrets and intentions.   After helping hundreds of people who have come my way asking for help in their efforts to heal from divorce—a fact I consider a gift of Divine design—I knew, finally, that I had to write the book myself.

Note to Divorcing Individuals or Couples without Children

If you are a divorcing individual or part of a couple who either have no children or whose children are adults, off on their own, perhaps even with children of their own, this book is also for you! Although I have focused on families with children in the following stories, the fact is that many of the formats the adults use in the rituals here are totally applicable to adults for whom sharing a Divorce Ritual with offspring is not an issue. You can find tools for doing a ritual with the person you shared marriage or a primary relationship with. You can also find ideas for doing a ritual *without* your ex-partner, either by yourself or with friends.

The format Roger and Andrea used—sharing affirmations and letting go of old angers and hurts—for their part in the ritual in Chapter 1 offers a model for anyone divorcing who wishes to focus on re-valuing what good has been gained and is being taken from the relationship and/or letting go of the past. Couples can share an experience that makes way for them to forgive each other, find a constructive path to freedom, and, in some cases, lay a foundation for transforming a committed relationship into a friendship. Essentially, such rituals can offer couples a rite of passage for beginning their separate lives.

There is another form of Affirmations in Chapter 7 (p. 118) you may use as a model. Another form of affirmations may be seen in Chapter 9 (pp. 148-149). You may also find the Statements in Chapter 3—Setting Intentions—a useful tool (see pp. 64-66). You may also want to consider writing a letter to yourself, as in Chapter 11 (see p. 179-180). If you read the ritual a divorcing woman shares with her friends in Chapter 4—in which she states regrets, what she still values, and what she intends to do and be in the future (pp. 76-79, 81-82)—you may find several or all of those parts to be adaptable to your circumstances. Or, you might wish to write vows to yourself, if you want to focus on moving forward in newly empowered ways, as you might see in Chapter 5 (p. 95-96), Chapter 10 (pp. 169-170), or Chapter 12 (p. 192). You may, in fact, want to adapt portions of a number of rituals in this book's stories—if they suit your needs and situation.

Perusing the Guidelines at the end of each chapter may provide you with a number of valuable suggestions, which you may use as springboards for your own creative diving into your truths.

Introduction

Must We Say We Did Not Love?

ultures throughout the world make much of marriage—
a symbol of continuity for the society, survival of the species.
The ceremony of marriage is one of the high sacred rituals in
most countries, in virtually all spiritual communities. As the
community's affirmation of the private commitment two
people are making, a wedding is rightfully a deeply meaningful ritual. But for far too many, the wedding itself has
become the obligatory and often perfunctory, yet incredibly
expensive, preface to an elaborate party, also astonishingly
expensive. Even with such commercial extravagance, most
weddings perform important spiritual and/or social functions
for the partners being married. Most people I know, myself
included, felt that they could not feel more committed to
their partner than they already did at the time of their
wedding. Yet somehow the wedding itself, the bonding of
vows before witnesses and the community affirmation for
those vows, did actually deepen the commitment. It clearly

is a crucial marking of a personal and communal passage.

We do not have, in any culture or any spiritual community I know of, a comparable, consistently practiced, ritual for divorce. One might wonder: Why would anyone *want* to have a ceremony for a "failed" marriage, when each person involved may be angry or bitter, when one person may be glad to be gone while the other is devastated?

Yet, historically, societies around the globe have traditions for ceremony in times of pain and loss as well as times of joy. Funerals, ceremonies at the time of death, are probably the other most common ritual across cultures. The funeral can serve an important function even for those who had a difficult relationship with the deceased. While we may miss a loved one for the rest of our lives, a funeral still offers a time to come to terms with the death, say goodbye, and prepare to go on with our own lives.

For some, after having a funeral—or, in some cases, instead of it—a wake, an informal memorial gathering in honor of the person, is a form of ritual that furthers the process of transition. With its combination of "toasts" and "roasts," a wake affords us time to remember the whole person: his or her character, strengths, weaknesses, idiosyncrasies, and talents. We can share what irritated us to distraction, what we loved best, and how the person's own unique spirit radiated through it all. Such an experience elicits both tears and laughter.

Most ritual is designed to *move us* in some way. In

Church, it may be to move us into closer connection with the Divine, toward some part of our own true nature. It may be to move us to seek forgiveness for hurting another person. In Nature, simple rituals, such as sitting quietly beside a creek or walking along a mountain trail, may connect us to our Mother Earth and/or the all-encompassing Universal Spirit. We may tap into a source of strength we thought was depleted. The ritual of the pre-game tailgate party can serve the purpose of bringing friends together, hyping up the supporters' energy for the big game. Whether in church, in nature, or at the football game, I believe that ritual is a powerful tool for transitions.

As society changes, I think we must adapt to meet the evolving needs people have for rituals of transition. My contention is that in our day, because divorce and the breakups of long-term commitments are so commonplace, we need ritual for acknowledging the psycho-spiritual significance of divorce—of ceasing our commitment. A divorce might be seen as the death of a relationship, or at least the death of a relationship as it existed before. We might never see the other person again. We may remain connected for the rest of our lives through our children—whether we want to or not.

Whatever our circumstances, it is profoundly damaging to make a promise and then, finding that one is unable and/or unwilling to keep it, to simply walk away, without a process for marking and facilitating the transition, both for each individual and the community that is impacted.

Imagine, if when someone died, we just got up the next day and went to work? What if there were no process, spiritual or secular, available for making the transition or coming to terms with the finality of that death?

That void is what our culture offers people who get divorced or who end committed relationships. A giant hoopla for their commitment, but then nothing to aid the transition at the end of the commitment except embarrassment, shame, silence, pointed or indirect reproaches, active criticism, anger and despair, spoken or unspoken bitterness, and sadness.

Another important point, I think, is that the lack of ritual for divorcing couples and families signifies society's lack of recognition of divorce as a legitimate fact of our lives. This lack keeps divorce locked in a box called "failure." While I see relationship commitments and marriage as sacred, and believe it worth working hard to keep them healthy, there are times when divorce can be the best thing for a couple or a family. A couple may have married in their early 20s and have no interests in common by the time they're 35. A divorce from an abusive, alcoholic, or drug-dependent person may be essential to the health of the partner and any children, no matter how much they may love the person. I believe we need to normalize divorce instead of seeing it as failure; we must make divorce a healthy process for marriages that still prove to be unhealthy or unfulfilling even after appropriate effort has been put into sustaining them.

There is currently substantive effort in this direction. I am particularly grateful for the growth of the International Academy of Collaborative Professionals, a group that is becoming a worldwide movement of therapists, mediators, family law attorneys, judges, coaches, realtors, and financial planners who work together to guide couples and families through a divorce process in a "collaborative," non-adversarial manner, in ways that ensure both adults and children emerge as whole as possible.

Whatever society's response, the people getting a divorce, or separating after a non-legal but long-held commitment, and the people who love them all suffer because, for most, ending a committed relationship hurts deeply, regardless of how it is carried out. And we have not developed ceremonies or rituals that could more effectively ease that suffering. Many people go to couple's counseling in the final stages of problematic relationships; there they may say final words in the presence of the therapist. Some people have their last words in court. A few intentionally go to closure counseling, to say all that needs to be said in a fair environment. But even fewer know how to mark the emotional, psychological, and/or spiritual crises that such a finality creates.

I have concluded that these and many other endings or closures *are* spiritual crises, and most people don't know how to honor and heal their pain or feelings of loss, or how to express their resolve to move on. I have found that creating an individually appropriate ritual or ceremony to mark that commitment to healing can be transformative.

I have helped many couples and families create meaningful rituals for the end of primary relationships. For virtually every one of them, it was the first ritual of that kind they'd ever heard of, much less created and participated in. In every single case, the people involved indicated that having a ceremony to mark both the end and a new beginning was crucial to their healing, to their ability to move on in strength to the next phases of their lives.

What *Is* Ritual?

What exactly is a *ritual*? The word itself is defined in several different ways. Even in the Oxford English Dictionary, most definitions are limited and narrow. Here are two: "A formal or symbolic act or observance or a series of them as on religious or state occasions" and "a sacred ceremony repeated at regular intervals." The words "ceremony" and "sacred" are frequently used in defining ritual. *Ceremony* is described as "a prescribed form or method for the performance of a religious or solemn ceremony," and *sacred* as "set apart or dedicated to religious use," "pertaining to hallowed things or places," "consecrated by love or reverence," and "entitled to reverence or respect."

As I have reflected on these definitions, and many others, I find that the further down the list I go from the primary denotative meanings, the closer I get to words that carry a fuller meaning of ritual: the words "symbolic," "form," "hallowed places," "consecrated," "dedicated," "purpose," "reverence," and "respect."

The image that, for me, holds the essential nature of ritual is a coming together of these elements:

1) the selection of a space that has special meaning,
2) intentionally planning what we want to say and do in a time set apart just for that,
3) making clear commitments that are set in a context of respect for ourselves and others, and
4) using meaningful words and special objects to symbolize those commitments.

Together, these components of ritual form a process that can engage a participant's body, mind, spirit, and actions in ways that have great power. This *gestalt* (the unified effect of the whole) can facilitate spontaneous and genuinely new insights.

Yet I know there remains a problem: many people still resist the idea of *doing ritual*. And I think there is good reason for that resistance.

The History and Reputation of Ritual

Many of the definitions of *ritual* focus on religious or governmental *ceremony*. Moreover, the tone of some of the definitions of ceremony that I did not include earlier is less than inviting to our contemporary ears: "The doing of some forced act in the manner prescribed by authority… " and "to stand on ceremony" is to "observe convention," focusing on "mere outward form." Being controlled by others, forced to participate in formal activities totally lacking in spirit and spontaneity—sound fun? Not to me!

Ritual's stifling reputation is certainly deserved in many settings. Whereas in tribal nations, ritual was something in which everyone participated actively, today, leaders in many institutions, religious or civil, determine and direct ritual and ceremony. For those who identify with the meaning of the symbolism, the words and actions of those ceremonies, such ritual will have great power and meaning (witness the huge television audience for a state wedding or funeral—or the Super Bowl!). Unfortunately huge numbers of people no longer feel actively engaged in any ritual or ceremony in which they have participated.

For many people in our society, the very word *ritual* has come to be associated with rejected forms. *Ritual* has come to mean words repeated by rote, actions one does without thinking (perfunctory genuflecting or chanting mantras), songs or hymns one sings whose lyrics have meanings they don't believe. For people who have left traditional spiritual communities because ritual acts have ceased to have meaning, *ritual* becomes synonymous with offensive content, mindless actions, and hierarchy. That, however, is not the heart of ritual; that is the result of ritual losing its heart.

Many of us in the United States do not have any affiliation with a church, synagogue, mosque, temple, spiritual community, or tribe—not even a coherent, solid cluster of intimate friends. Thus, we have no community of people close at hand in those very times when we need to feel that we are not alone. Put in more concrete terms, only fifty percent of the population of this country cites affiliation with a religion of any kind (however limited) in the current census, and in many cities the percentage is much smaller. What we must remember, I think, is that neither a religion that is not meeting our needs nor a totally secular science can fulfill spiritual needs, and many people are suffering in the midst of this transitional crisis.

How Can We Envision Ritual With a Heart?

I've chosen to use the word *ritual* instead of some other word, such as closure, primarily because I believe it is important to reclaim ritual's power, attest to its essential function in our psycho-spiritual health, and wrest it from its rather pervasive negative connotations. Ritual, as envisioned by sages in virtually every culture on earth, is created and observed by making some space sacred, in which an individual or a group marks the significance of the gathering in ways that *fully engage* every participant. Through ritual, the relationship of the entire community is deepened and the relationship of every individual to whatever he or she considers sacred— Great Spirit, Mother Earth, a pantheon of gods and goddesses, God, Goddess, Allah, Self, Humanity, or the teachings of Buddha—is affirmed. Ritual *is* often repetitive in the sense that a community may gather repeatedly over time to perform ceremony, but *not* inherently repetitious in the sense of droning, mumbling mindlessness. At the same time, a ritual does not have to be repeated to be life-changing.

How can we re-envision ritual so that it will have integrity and personal significance for us, whatever our past relationship with it has been? I believe we must do just what our ancestors did *before* the prescribed forms existed. Create sacred space and share expressions that make sense to us and our chosen community's shared beliefs. Our "community" may be ourselves alone, reflecting on our place in the Universe, or it may include one other person, a group of friends, a spiritual body, or a large gathering of strangers with a common intent to unite in a thoughtful, caring way. Doing that *is* creating ritual.

I reclaim the process of ritual-making in my work because I know from long experience there is inherent wisdom in the *gestalt* of ritual. Ritual, thoughtfully created and fully engaged in, has heart, so much heart that it heals when nothing else can. I've seen it happen over and over again. Although part of ritual's power remains essentially mysterious, I believe we can understand some things about its process that will help us realize why we need to restore it to its proper place in our lives.

Why Is a Divorce Ritual Needed?

You may wonder, "Why doesn't it work just as well to go

to a therapist?" "What can a ritual do that therapy doesn't do?" "Can't I get all the support I need from my friends?" Therapists often see clients who have, in many respects, successfully worked through their feelings about a relationship of an issue, and then continue to stay "stuck" as if they can't pull themselves free to move on with their life.

Even people who have received extensive counseling can move, through ritual, beyond one of the most serious danger points in the therapeutic process: staying focused on the pain of the past and continuing to see themselves as victims. In her popular book, *Anatomy of the Spirit*, Caroline Myss refers to this way of being as "woundology." My experience leads me to conclude that making a ritual, especially when witnessed by another person, allows transition and release to occur in a *gestalt* of forward-moving action, "thawing" that "frozen" self-concept that may well be tied to the old relationship. Moreover, having a witness makes one more accountable and assists someone to move beyond seeing herself/ himself as a victim. Many mental health professionals who have referred clients to me have testified that ritual "concluded" a therapeutic process for the client in a more complete way than they had ever seen before. A synergy between   therapy and ritual is palpable.

Ritual is important for men, women, and children when couples and families separate. Both men and women in this culture, for different reasons, have a hard time realizing that active engagement in ritual can create movement necessary to heal their past. Often, when we begin working together, men frequently express the belief that a ritual "won't do any good," yet once they have experienced it, they express amazement at how important it actually felt. "I think you know I wasn't too keen on this idea," a hundred men have told me, "but I'm so glad we did it. I'm blown away by the impact it had. I *really* feel better."

Even if they are drawn to ritual, or feel the need to signify a passage in order to heal, women as well as men may dismiss it as "probably unnecessary, and maybe even silly." Children are different. Most of them still recognize instinctively the importance of marking significant moments of joy or sorrow. I have found many children who innately love ritual, however simply they enact it. They wave goodbye to the ocean before getting in the car to go home, make sure their pet hamster gets a proper burial, know you must say "I love you" and give a kiss goodnight to teddy bears and parents and grandmas. And the blankets have to be just so before the light goes out each night.

How is it that children instinctively recognize the importance of ritual for daily, ordinary passages while our culture as a whole generally ignores all but three surrounding birth, marriage, and death? Somehow between childhood and adulthood many people become convinced that most of life's passages are not worthy of mentioning, let alone of ritual. All too often I see children struggle to hold on to their innate "knowing" of ritual's power when the culture tries to stifle it in them, such as when a child of divorcing parents asked me, whispering in my ear, if it was weird that she wanted to bury a picture of her hugging parents in the backyard of the house they won't live in together anymore. Some young people still hold on with confidence. In the first chapter of this book, an 11-year-old boy tells his parents, "You had a wedding ceremony; aren't we going to do something for the divorce?" Prompted by their son, his parents contacted me to help them create a divorce ritual.

What Is a Divorce Ritual?

When I speak of a *divorce ritual*, I mean creating a sacred space and time to *name, honor, attend to,* and *release* the truths surrounding change, pain, and/or loss brought about by divorce as well as what remains true and/or valuable from the past. One also needs to *state one's intentions* for the future. I believe that a personally designed and meaningful ceremony asks us to bring our bodies, minds, emotions and spirits to account, fully present into a place of honor. It requires us to articulate that we need help to heal, and to affirm that we are not alone. And it gives us support to be safe enough, empowered enough to speak our truths and survive them. In turn, we will experience healing on a physical, mental, emotional, and spiritual level. Thus, as I see it, we *move* into the ritual space to *take action* about our anguish; those who gather with us *move* closer to *listen, affirm,* and *bear witness* to our *work.*

Within this framework, every ritual can be tailored to meet the needs of the people involved. Who participates and where it happens, what is done and said during the gathering varies dramatically, as you will see from the stories in the book. After each story, I highlight guidelines for how to create your own ritual.

Rather than throwing ritual out of our lives, we can re-educate ourselves about how to make it meaningful again, if indeed it has become "dead" to us. Many times people ask me the meaning of "symbols" they grew up with—why people throw flowers in a grave or pour handfuls of dirt over a coffin. They say they once "felt good" about them, but didn't know why. Others may find that certain forms they once loved, be they specific actions or symbolic acts, no longer seem appropriate or useful. We need to create forms of ritual that *are* useful and full of current meaning, rather than assume that ritual itself has no place in honoring the cycles of our lives.

I am heartened to see the increasing number of spiritual leaders and mental health professionals who are realizing that we too have neglected the importance of rites of passage for individuals locked in unresolved issues from the past, especially when the traditional cultural forms of acknowledgment do not fit.

Artists have long said that form and function must be connected—a bud vase and a coffee mug cannot be the same shape. Form will follow function or function will grow out of form. And so it is with the art of spiritual expression. All of us, male and female, young or old—however different or alike we may be—need to reclaim ritual as a vital container and vehicle for closing one cycle of our lives and opening to the healing and transformation that will usher us into the next.

Edna St. Vincent Millay, known to schoolchildren primarily as the poet who wrote of "burning the candle at both ends," also wrote some profoundly wise sonnets, among which was one that, in part, reads:

"Tell me why, my erstwhile dear, my no longer cherished,
  Must we say we did not love, just because it perished?"

For millions of people, those words can point the way to the heretofore unthinkable: that there is a way to divorce each other with the same mindful intention and civility that they showed-to each other in the beginning of their relationship. Millay's words embody the ethos for rituals of divorce, rituals that provide a way to affirm what was, that two people loved. At the same time, they acknowledge that, at least for one and perhaps for both, one species of love they shared did, in fact, perish. Whether a divorce is honored with a ritual by one person alone, a couple with or without a witness, some cluster or all of a family, or a divorcing family with their entire community of friends, it is my fervent belief that our society can be made healthier and kinder one such honored passage at a time.

CHAPTER 1

Amicable Divorce: A Ritual When a Couple Has Children

Andrea and Roger   Ryan, 11   Becca, 8   Charlie, 5

*O*ne day I received a call from a friend, a local therapist, regarding a couple she had been seeing for two years in therapy. She told me that the couple, Roger and Andrea, had decided—wisely, she thought—to divorce, but that they both had worked very hard to come to an amicable resolution because they wanted to "do right" by themselves, each other, and their three children. She said, "They want a ritual of divorce, and I haven't a clue how to advise them. Could I refer them to you?" I said I would be very willing to talk with them.

Within 24 hours, Andrea called me and we set an appointment for me to meet the family at their home. They greeted me warmly and introduced me to their three children, Ryan, Becca, and Charlie. Before I had a chance to sit down, Ryan asked, "Are you the lady that's going to help us do our ritual for Mom and Dad's divorce? It was my idea, you know. I've looked at Mom and Dad's wedding book ever since I was little, and I always imagined how they started our family with that celebration. If they're gonna get a divorce, I thought we should do something for that, too—with us kids in it."

I was impressed. "What a great idea, Ryan. I think you're a very wise young man, and I think it's great that your parents listened to you."

Charlie chimed in, "What's a rich'al?"

Becca sighed, with the slightly superior smile of a knowledgeable eight-year-old, "Mom and Dad already told us, we're …"

Roger laughed and interrupted her, "OK, OK, let's at least let her sit down first."

Watching the warm, lighthearted interactions between the adults and children in this family and the open spontaneity of these children, I experienced that knee-jerk thought, "What a *great* family! A divorce underway *here*?" But I know such impressions are often shaky.

We all talked for awhile, I told them what *ritual* is as I see it, and that I'd help their parents with some ideas so that they could talk over with them what they'd all like in their special ritual together. Then Andrea asked the kids to go play in the back yard while we adults talked.

Roger and Andrea settled into a more serious tone. They

seemed pleasant and resolute. I found out that he was a certified public accountant; she was a librarian. I asked if they wanted to tell me a little about their divorce. "It's certainly optional," I said, "but sometimes it helps to plan it if I have more context, some knowledge of the circumstances."

They nodded and Andrea said, "We are both 'nice' people, too nice really. We never want to hurt each other, or anybody else, so I think we get afraid to be honest. We both hate conflict. We never fight, but we've never really resolved hurt feelings or feelings of betrayal or disappointments, either. And they all build up over time if you don't clear the air.

Roger, who'd been nodding as she spoke, added, "Even though we can be nice to each other, we really want different things out of life. My life is pretty simple. Like, I love going to work, coming home, working in the garden, being with the kids, and maybe going for a hike or bike ride with the family on the weekend. Andrea has 8,000 things going on. She's on committees, chairs a local program to teach adults to read, and a bunch of other things. Plus, she loves to talk a lot, go out to plays and movies, discuss politics and current events. Frankly, it wears me out. I like to go to sleep early; she likes to stay up and read. There are times when I have a glass of wine in the back yard after work, and I wish she'd just be out there sitting with me. But then I know that if she comes out, she'll have ten topics to tell me about that will— I don't know—kind of shatter the peace and quiet. Then I hope she *doesn't* come out."

Andrea said, "And it's the opposite for me. I love going to plays and then going out afterward, having lively discussions. The peace Roger doesn't want shattered feels like walking underwater to me, like I'm in slow motion with some force holding me back. I get so frustrated and bored. We've finally realized, with our therapist's help, that the way we're living is so out of sync that it's painful to both of us. We haven't made love in so long I can't remember the last time. Must've been *sometime* before Charlie was born!" They both chuckled. "Even though we know that no marriage is perfect, neither of us wants to live the rest of our lives this way, wishing the other was different or would change."

Roger added, "We've always liked each other. I just think we're better friends than being a couple. I know that sounds strange, maybe, but our rhythms are so different. I think that as friends our differences were OK, we even liked it. But as a steady diet in a marriage, it just doesn't work."

Having heard all this, I understood why their therapist was supportive of their decision to divorce. This couple had articulated eloquently that sometimes an inexplicable alchemy makes a marriage work—or not.

After thinking a moment, I said, "It occurs to me that it might be hard for your kids to understand why you're getting a divorce, given that there hasn't been a lot of obvious conflict, from what you've said." They nodded. "Over time," I suggested, "I think it would be good, as they seem ready or interested, to give them enough information—just as you've explained it to me—so they can understand it. If they don't, they might have difficulty trusting their own relationships, wondering if something sort of 'invisible' might, at some point, make it all go wrong."

They looked at each other, nodding, then back at me.

"In my own family," I continued, "my parents were both ministers, and we had what our community saw as sort of 'the perfect family.' I never heard my parents argue, only once did I hear raised voices, and then, suddenly, my mother left and they weren't together anymore. It took me a long time to figure it all out."

Both Andrea and Roger reacted visibly. "You know," Andrea said, "we've already gotten that from some of our family and friends. Some understand, but others just don't get why we'd get a divorce. One of my friends said, 'If you guys get a divorce, none of us is safe!'" Roger added, looking again at Andrea, "We'll really take it seriously to make sure our kids learn to understand it."

When I turned the focus of the conversation to their divorce ritual, Roger said, "Even though it sounded strange to think our son would equate getting divorced with some ceremony like marriage, as soon as he suggested it, we realized immediately he was absolutely right. The kids need to be part of the dissolution of our marriage at the same time we're affirming we'll always be family in the sense of being their parents, looking out for their best interests together."

Clearly, he and Andrea had discussed this at length because she nodded while he was speaking. He said, "It's really comforting to me somehow to know that other people are marking divorces this way, I don't know why."

I replied, "I think the fact that more and more people are doing divorce rituals represents a movement in parts of our society to get beyond 'the blame game' into acknowledging that evolution, change, is part of a cycle as natural as the seasons, even in many cases of divorce. A Divorce Ritual offers you all a means to make a positive, empowering transition instead of settling for the way so many people do it, walking away from a marriage simply feeling like a failure."

I went on, "I think that two profoundly important things need to happen in your ritual. First, you, as the adults, need to acknowledge the end of your relationship as married spouses, partners. That needs to be firm, and at the same time said in a way that has a positive tone of moving forward rather than focusing on pain and loss. I know that with kids the pain and loss will be dealt with many times, but the function of the ritual is to create a container of transition in a more empowering way. Second," I went on, "you and the children need to reaffirm the continuation of your relationship as parents and children. This paradox is central, I believe, to one of the most significant crises that many people face, both parents and children. Yet, most divorcing parents don't honor this passage in any way that matches the solemnity and communal sharing that surrounded their wedding. Nor do they consistently include their children in their work toward closure and transition." After setting this context, one of the primary questions I asked was, "What are the most important gifts you would like to give the children through this ritual?"

Andrea answered, "I want them to know we'll always be there for them, and that both of our houses will be home." They had already assured the children that they would share custody, so there would be no need for the children to choose one parent over the other. She went on, "I want them to know there are things we still like about each other, and I think they need to know clearly they have not done anything wrong. Even though we've already told them that a hundred times, I think they still worry."

Roger added, "I agree with everything Andrea said, and I'd also like for the kids to be able to express whatever they need to about their feelings. I'd like to ask them what they want in the ritual, get their input. I think we could really use your experience on this. And I'd like for you to be there with us to facilitate this, oversee it. Plus, I think the kids would think it's official to have a minister there."

We discussed many different ways to symbolize this transition in relationships within "family." I proposed the possibility of burying something to signify closure and planting bulbs to signify a belief in the future as a family, and we agreed on an outline. They said they'd talk to the kids and get back to me, and I asked them to choose a site based on their needs and the children's comfort.

A week later, we all gathered in the backyard of the home they had lived in for twelve years. Roger and Andrea asked me to come a half-hour before the ceremony to spend some time with the children, so I was able to visit with each of them again. They were all talkative, engaged kids. Then Ryan, the eleven-year-old, said, "Even though this was all my idea, now I'm kinda nervous."

"I think that's natural any time we do something we haven't done before. No one will have to do or say *anything* they don't choose to."

Becca bounced around, and Charlie picked up and threw pebbles. So I said, "I'll explain everything we're doing as we go along, but if you have any questions, please ask! The most important thing is that you understand, so you can remember later, what we're saying and doing. Some things we say and do may make you feel like laughing, or you might feel sad or angry. It's all OK. All feelings are allowed." The whole family agreed, nodding seriously.

Once we sat down together on the grass in a circle, everyone settled in. It wasn't so different from a picnic. Birds came and went from the feeder, the flowers in their garden gave off their scents in the light breeze, and the sun, pleasantly warm, felt good on our backs, chests and shoulders. Charlie started picking at the grass.

I began, "Today we've come together here to honor this

family in a time of change. Thirteen years ago, Roger and Andrea, you made some promises that you need to let go of today. Yet your promises to care about each other, love your children and be the best parents you can possibly be are absolutely for keeps. We are having this ceremony so that you as parents and kids can mark both what is changing and what is NOT changing."

The children were listening intently. "Let's begin by having you, Roger and Andrea, say what you value about each other today."

Roger started. "Andrea," he began, "I value your kind heart, your gentleness with the kids, the way you always make birthdays special, and the way you cook way better than I do (the kids laughed, and Ryan interjected, 'That's not hard, Dad!'). I really like the way you pick great books for all of us to read. I respect the way you live by your values and your passion for working in our community, how you put your politics into action that makes a difference. I'm grateful that you're still my friend, and I know we'll always be connected by our children." Becca's eyes got wide and teary when Roger's voice broke, but she clearly kept listening.

Andrea said, "Roger, I value your intelligence, your head for money, and your commitment to being a dad. I value your hard work taking care of the yard—so beautiful right now because of all of your many weekends of mowing and planting and weeding and mulching ('Hey, Mom,' Ryan blurted, 'we helped with that, too!' to which Andrea said, 'I'm not forgetting that—I'll thank you for that later, I promise, but I'm just talking about Dad now'). I'm glad you're the kind of man who shows his feelings." She had tears in her eyes as she turned to me to indicate that she had finished.

"Having said what you value about each other, how about if you tell each of your children what you value about them?"

They took turns this time, spontaneously, focusing on each child by age, youngest first. They thanked Charlie for his fantastic curiosity, about everything, and for how much they had learned because of his questions, and they said they hoped he would never stop asking questions. They told him how much they loved his laugh and how often he got the whole family laughing. And they thanked him for his hugs, his sloppy kisses, and his commitment to cleaning his hamster cage ("Ewwww," Becca involuntarily groaned, eliciting a sock from Charlie), and told him they would always love him.

They thanked Becca for her great love of everything she does—spending time with her friends, her ballet lessons, even her schoolwork. They appreciated how she had taught the whole family how to have better posture. They said she was one of the kindest people they knew, and they were proud of her for that. They also told her they admired how she did things that scared her—like learning how to dive off the high board at the swim club last summer. Their hope for her was that she stay happy and focused on what she loved and that they would always love her.

They thanked Ryan for his taking his responsibilities as the big brother so seriously. They thanked him for his help with projects such as the lawn mowing, weeding, and garbage collection, his brilliance on the computer and his amazing ability with puzzles. They thanked him for suggesting the terrific idea of having this ritual. Their hope for him was that he know for sure he was absolutely great and that they loved him forever.

Listening to the appreciations these parents gave to each other and their children, one might still ask, "Now, tell me again, why in the world are *these* people getting a divorce?" They still *liked* each other! They could speak respectfully, even lovingly. However, what often gets lost in the divorce process is all the things family members did and still do value in each other. Bringing focus to what is valued can transform the energy in the midst of divorce. And, as my earlier conversation with Andrea and Roger had underscored, anyone outside a relationship can *never* really know what goes on behind closed doors.

At this point in this family's divorce ritual, the kids seemed subdued, but clearly they were also buoyed by the affirmations from their folks. I asked them if they wanted to say affirmations to their parents, but Ryan spoke for all of them and said, "We decided we'd write a letter to Mom and Dad together tonight before we go to bed about what we love about each of them. We want to do it that way, OK?"

"Absolutely fine!" I assured them. "Whatever way you want to do this is exactly right."

Roger and Andrea had three beautifully wrapped packages that they presented to their children. Unwrapping them, the children found a tennis bracelet with their initials on top and "Family Forever—Mom and Dad" inscribed on the back. Each child also received two brand new keys, one gold and one silver, on a key ring. The gold one was the key to Mom's house, the silver one to Dad's. Andrea said, "We want you to know always that we are family forever, and that your home will always be wherever you have a key. You will always have a key to both of our homes." Loudly admiring their presents as they put them on, the children clearly grasped the significance of their gifts.

The next part of the ritual addressed that vital aspect of any separation—letting go. Out of my tote bag I took a burlap sack in which I had assorted bulbs and some paper. I told the children, "I asked your folks if we could do this and got their OK. We're going to do what I call 'a burial of hard feelings' today with the hope of a brighter tomorrow. When there's a divorce, it's natural that there are some angers, some sadness, hard feelings. Your parents have those feelings, you kids probably do, too. We believe it's healthy to speak those emotions.

"Today, though, in this ritual, we're going to say the truth just to ourselves because you have already told each other how you're feeling at other times. We're planting bulbs as a symbol of trust. I plant a bulb, trusting it will flower next spring as a crocus or a tulip or a daffodil or a narcissus. In the same way, even though we may have hard feelings about this divorce, we can still move forward knowing that the hard feelings don't make you stop caring about each other, and that the future will come with you five still loving each other.

"Here are some scraps of paper. Write down anything you're angry or mad about because of this divorce. When you've written it all down, you're going to bury the paper and put a bulb on top of it. The paper, which is actually special compost paper, is heavy enough to write on but will still help the bulb grow into a flower that will bloom next spring. Then, when you see the flowers, you can think about your feelings and notice how they've shifted. We hope it'll help you remember how all the feelings we experience as a family can be used to grow. Charlie, I'll help you write what you think, OK?" Ready for the task, he scooted closer so he could whisper in my ear.

Each person took a batch of pieces of paper, a pen or pencil, and started to write. Ryan and Becca both said they liked that they could tell the truth on the paper and then bury it. Roger had the bulb planters and the bone meal handy, so when each person had a "hard feeling" written down, she or he took a bulb, dug a hole, placed the paper and the bone meal in the bottom of the hole, placed the bulb on top of it, and replaced the dirt over the hard feeling and the bulb. Everyone was busy, quietly focused, and quite a few bulbs got planted.

When everyone was finished, Roger said, "How does that feel?"

"Good," said Ryan, "I'm glad I didn't have to say it out loud. I know you've heard me scream enough anyway."

"Good—and sad," Becca added. "This is the part I really hate." Her mom and dad nodded but did not rush to "fix" her feelings.

"I dug it!" crowed Charlie, ever the clown, and he got the response he desired—groans and laughter. "Actually, I buried a lot of stuff, didn't I?" As his scribe, I nodded.

Ryan said, "Let's take pictures!" He clearly had particular groupings in mind from his long-time attachment to the wedding album. So, I took pictures of Roger and Andrea alone, Roger and Andrea with each child, Roger and Andrea in the back row with the three children in front, and all five of them in a row. For the grand finale we had a shot of all of them *and* the four family pets—a dog, two cats, and a hamster. By the time the photo session was finished, the entire family was joking around with each other, and three kids wore shiny new tennis bracelets on their wrists.

Guidelines for Divorce Rituals for Couples with Children

1. Decide whether you need an experienced facilitator to guide the ritual or if you have the ability to do the ritual without one.

   a. This is vital because it is important not to take on something that could become unmanageable emotionally for any member of the family.

   b. You will need to take into consideration the needs of each member of the family regarding having an "outsider" present.

2. Create a ritual that is workable for all family members and takes into account:

   a. The level of conflict or cooperation the parents have with each other so a ritual can be created that honors the realities of the relationship. This complex reality may create the need for separate or several rituals; i.e., each adult may choose to have one ritual with a support group, where different truths can be spoken, and another with children present.

   b. The different beliefs family members may have about what an acceptable ritual would be.

   c. The children's ages, emotional states, and cognitive levels.

3. Respect the capacity children have for ritual and for adapting in constructive ways when change occurs.

4. Recognize that a key goal of a divorce ritual for a family with children is to provide the children with a tangible form for understanding and feeling their parents' commitment to:

   a. Interact without using the children as pawns in their conflicts.

   b. Provide for their children's continued physical and emotional security after the divorce.

5. Ask the children what they would like to have included in the ritual. For Ryan, "divorce pictures" were crucial to making a secure transition.

6. Make sure everyone knows what will be included in the ritual ahead of time so adults and children alike are emotionally prepared.

7. Make the ritual flexible so people can have different degrees of participation, or simply be a part of it without saying anything.

8. Addressing the painful feelings with honesty, while recognizing that the ritual is not-like a therapy session might be-for the purpose of processing those feelings; its primary purpose is to create a transition that offers healing.

   a. As in the ritual described here, the feelings of anger, hurt and loss can be written rather than discussed out loud.

b. It is helpful to provide children and adults with a process for beginning to release and transform feelings of anger and bitterness. In this case, burying the paper with their thoughts and feelings along with a bulb that will grow into something beautiful accomplished that goal.

c. Make a space that is safe for tears as well as laughter, simply as an expression of "what is" in the moment.

9. Carefully select whether to focus on the appreciations or the anger and hurt first. It is often wise to focus on the positive first and then focus on the hurt and anger as part of what it being let go, as was done here.

10. Make discussion of positive feelings realistic so it is believable. Making the positive conversation focus on appreciations is one very effective way to do this.

a. Make sure the ritual affirms what was there, at the same time it acknowledges that a transition has occurred to something else.

b. Make sure no one feels obliged to say anything they don't feel.

11. If possible, provide tangible symbols for the children that remind them of their own security and something positive to look forward to. In this case, the tennis bracelets, key rings, and the bulbs all served that   purpose.

12. If the parents are open to the idea, introduce the concept that you all still have family ties even if the parents no longer live together. The affirmations and sentiments in

the tennis bracelets, "Family Forever-Mom and Dad," both conveyed this message.

13. Above all, make the ritual represent realistically what the parents can commit to in making the transition. For some parents, a commitment to not arguing in front of the children and/or not telling them negative things about the other parent may be the best they can offer.

CHAPTER 2

Hostile Divorce: Each Parent Has a Separate Ritual with the Children

Lyle and Laura   *Brian, 12*   *Katie, 11*   *Jessica, 8*

*S*ometimes a divorcing couple cannot get past their rage, hurt, disappointment or other debilitating emotions enough to work together for their children's benefit. Perhaps the divorce is acrimonious, or perhaps they have decided that it's best for their emotional well-being to have their only communication be through their attorneys. But the anguish of their children, evident whether both parents are with the children or not, may be of great concern to the attorneys, therapists, or caregivers involved. There is often someone who says, "These kids need closure! Who's thinking about the kids?"

It was an attorney who called me with such a situation. She said, "Monza, I heard you speak about divorce rituals at a conference not long ago, and I wonder if a situation I'm in might be one you could help me with. I am dealing with a divorce that's pretty brutal. I was talking with the wife, who's my client, in her home, and her 12-year-old son kept interrupting our meeting. He was being rude and demanding with his mother, tattling on his sister, turning the TV up so loud we couldn't hear ourselves think, just generally 'acting out' how pissed he is. After cautioning him several times to watch his mouth, my client burst into tears and said, 'I don't know what I'm going to do about Brian! He's never been like this! He's driving me absolutely nuts!' Then, Brian, who heard her, ran upstairs, slamming his bedroom door so hard it actually broke off the hinges. I'm no therapist, but I think this kid's in trouble."

First I recommended a fantastic therapist trained especially to deal with adolescents. She said, "I don't know if the kid'll agree to go, but I'll sure tell the mother. Brian's totally belligerent as right now."

Then I said, "If and when the time is right, and you think this family would benefit from some sort of ritual, please know I'll do anything I can to help. As a child of divorce myself, I know something of what the kids might be going through." She assured me she'd keep me informed.

I didn't hear from Wilda for a couple of months. But when she called the next time she said, "I wanted to give you an update on the family I was telling you about when we talked last: Brian has been seeing the guy you recommended. He's really doing better, not being so hard on his mom, for one thing—but, more important, he's being a lot more communicative about his anger. Also, the mom and I have been talking about the need to put a 'final stamp' on the divorce for the kids now that the decree is about to be signed. She likes the idea of some kind of ceremony, but she's adamant that she won't do it with the kids' dad. She can't stand to be in the same room with him! When I suggested it might be good if each parent did a ritual with the kids, she scoffed at the idea, saying 'Lyle's too passive to step up and do something like that! He's not going to go out of his way for the kids—he'll probably find excuses to not even do his visitation.' But she didn't object to having you talk to his attorney to see if there's any chance he'd do it. Do you think you'd be willing to talk with each of them if his attorney and I can set something up with Lyle?"

I said that I would and a week later I heard from Wilda again. "Lyle's attorney just called me and said Lyle is very willing to have his own 'divorce ceremony' with his kids, and he's just as ticked at his ex-wife as she is at him (no news to us). If you'd call him, he'd be grateful for any help. Here's his number, and my client's number, too."

I called Lyle right away, not wanting to let his readiness wane. And, from the start of our conversation, I liked him.

"I hear you're the Spiritually Healthy Divorce Guru!" he quipped.

After I finished laughing, I replied, "Guru I ain't, but I do care passionately about divorcing families. I'm a child of one myself, and even though I was 19 at the time, my sister was only 13, I know a good bit about the issues everyone can be going through."

"Was your parents' divorce as hateful as ours?" he asked.

"My parents were so mad at each other that when I graduated with my Master's, they never bothered to check and see which one of them was going to give me a ride to the party after the ceremony; they both jealously assumed I would have asked the other, and I was left back at the stadium with no ride!"

Lyle laughed hard. "I can just see Laura and me doin' something like that! Are things still that bad between them?"

"No, we all communicate with each other now—25 years later. My folks will never be friends, but they can be civil to each other if they have to be in the same space. That was *not* always the case, I'll tell ya! Lately, I've noticed that they actually sound compassionate when they ask me how the other is doing. Part of what's so important to me in this work is to find ways that help divorcing parents get over the intensity of their anger at each other so it doesn't drag on for years—because most parents end up having some ongoing connection for the rest of their lives, even if it's just through what they hear from their kids.

"Oh, no! Save me from such a fate! " Lyle groaned. "Well, I guess it *is* some comfort to know we're not the only couple to screw up our kids, and that there might be a little hope down the line for getting past this dead end we're at right now! Sounds like you've 'been there, done that, got that T-shirt.' That's good enough for me. So, you want to help me talk to my kids?"

I replied, "I'm sure you'll find your own way to talk with them, but I will do what I can to help you create some sort of acknowledgment of what's going on from your perspective— things that will change and what won't change in your relationship with them during and after the divorce."

"Sounds good," he said. "I'm way out of my depth here. I talk a good game because I'm a salesman, but I'm not good at all at talking about my feelings. Probably a big part of the reason Laura and I are getting a divorce, and why it's been so damn hard. I'd always shut down when things got rough, then she'd badger me 'til I'd blow up, then we'd have an argument, then I'd shut down again, and she be at me some more, on and on like that."

I asked, "Do you think I would judge you?"

"Hmm ... Yeah, maybe."

"Well, I'm glad I asked, then. I don't feel any judgment of you, Lyle. I've ended relationships myself in difficult ways, and I don't believe I'm in any position to judge how your life was with your ex-wife. I believe no one outside can ever know how we co-create patterns we find we ultimately can't live with."

"That's a good way to put it."

Many times I have worked with a divorcing couple and

thoroughly enjoyed both of them; but the dynamic between the two of them was hurtful to both people. I could already tell this would be such a situation.

I went on, "I do know, Lyle, that I wish my folks had communicated with us more skillfully when they were going through their divorce. They were so wrapped up in their own feelings that they stopped really being parents to us. My sister and I basically healed ourselves, or at least just had each other to talk to."

"Yeah, well, I want to do whatever I can to keep Brian, Katie, and Jessica from being any more miserable than they are."

"That's what's important. So, Lyle, what do you most want to say to your kids?"

"That I love them every bit as much as I did on the days they were born, that I'll always love them because they're my babies, will be even when they're grown up, and that I want them to know I'm there for 'em even though they're living primarily with their mom. I'm as close as the phone or e-mail. And I want to be there for their school stuff, sports stuff, recitals, and they need to tell me what's coming up so that I don't miss important events."

"Those all sound great, be sure to write it down. Now, they'll probably ask how you can promise to love them forever when you don't love their mom anymore."

"Yeah, you're right about that. They are thinking that now, I'm sure. I'll need to talk about that. What else?"

"Do you want to say something about being open to hearing what they're feeling, what they're going through, what they need to make them feel better?"

"OK, I can see that they would need to hear that. Just a sec', I'm writing this down."

After pausing, I added, "Think also about where you'd like to do this. Make it someplace special, but not 'out to dinner.' Being in public sometimes makes it hard for kids to express their feelings. Or even to hear yours. They get embarrassed, especially if they're young like yours, if they feel they're going to cry, or if they do. Or, if they need to speak loudly, if they show their anger. You don't want them to feel it's not OK for them to feel any of their feelings."

"Good point," Lyle replied. "We could take a hike and sit down at a vista point. We've hiked a lot together."

"Excellent. The only other thing I've found significant is saying something about how you will or won't talk about their mom. The reason for that is so they'll feel secure, and not worry about loyalty issues. Also you might give them some token of your constancy in being their dad."

"Whew," Lyle blew out a sigh. "That'll be a challenge, won't it? But I get what you mean about their security. And, yeah, I can find a gift for each of them. I always give them something for Father's Day anyway, we've had that tradition for their whole lives for Mother's and Father's Day, because we've told them we wouldn't have been a mother or a father without them."

"Well, it looks to me like you've already got an outline. Feel free to call me if you need anything else. And let me know how it goes, will you? It matters to me."

When I called his wife, Laura, she responded immediately. "Wilda told me you'd be calling, and I'm grateful. But I don't know where to begin."

I said, "That's understandable. You're going through a lot. I don't know whether or not Wilda told you that I'm a child of divorced parents, and the divorce was not an amicable one either. So I know how painful is and hope I can support you. Let's start by having you tell me what you'd like to accomplish by having some sort of 'divorce ritual' with your kids."

She thought awhile, then said, "Even though the kids and I talk all the time, and I hear all their rants and wails about how we're ruining their lives, I know a ritual would be different than a regular family meeting to talk specifically about how I want for us to hold this crisis in our hearts."

"Have they heard your feelings?"

"They've heard them, but not in exactly the best form," she sighed. "Sometimes they hear me crying after reading another letter from Lyle's attorney. Or talking to my best friend on the phone, trying not to raise my voice too much, but getting angrier and angrier, so it *does* get loud. I know the kids hear more than they should, there's no way to really hide how upset I am. Stuff like that. I've been trying not to let them see me completely fall apart, but sometimes it just happens."

"Do you believe they'll think you're weak if they see or hear you cry?"

"No, I think they are more likely to think I'm a bitch, because Lyle was so withholding and I complained that he wouldn't ever talk about things, and now they still hear me complain to friends. I guess it's silly to worry about what they hear now—they've heard it all before!" I could hear her choke back a sob.

I paused a moment, not wanting to rush forward when she was being so honest with me. "Laura, can you hear me if I say something right now?"

"Yes," she whispered, "I wish you would."

"I believe that kids are capable of understanding paradoxes, things that seem opposite when both parts are true. I believe that while your children *have* seen your relationship with their dad in whatever ways they've interpreted it, your children also see you holding the family together, running your home, getting their meals and their clothes clean and their homework done. And whether they think about that right now or not, that's strong. Especially now, when you're hurting. They may have feelings about your and Lyle's relationship, and those feelings will come out, but I don't believe that, whatever those feelings are, they have to be one way or another—either you are all strong or all weak. You're a human being, and being fully human is the best example you can give a growing child.

Just for the record, I wish my parents had not hidden their whole process, their range of feelings and capacities, from me in many ways that they did."

"Are you just being kind?" Laura asked shyly.

"Absolutely not. I'm telling you my most profound beliefs."

Changing the subject, Laura asked, "So, Monza, what constitutes a 'ritual' in your mind?"

I told her and answered the rest of her questions.

"Thanks, I think I can take it from here. At least I hope so, but I'll call if I get stuck. You've been very helpful."

I didn't hear from Lyle or Laura for awhile, although I thought of them from time to time, held them in my thoughts and prayers. Ironically, though, after a month I heard from both of them within days of each other.

Lyle said: "I had a great talk with my kids. Up on the top of Mt. Pisgah. We sat down and I said, 'Know how you can see all over the valley from up here? Well, I hope some day we'll be able to look over this hard time from the big perspective, where it all looks smaller than it feels today. But I know that for me, and prob'ly for you too, everything feels really big right now, like each house when you're in it. Anyway, there are some things I want to say to you' … and then I said what I talked to you about."

"Sounds fantastic, Lyle. How did the kids respond?"

"It was amazing. We all—all four of us—really talked.

After I made my promises to them, and told them I always wanted to hear what they're feeling, they told me what they're feeling right now. And it was Jessica, the little one, who started. I'll tell you, she sure didn't spare my feelings, but she told the truth, and it started the way for the others. It was all good ... even though some of it was hard, it was all good. And they loved the 'Un-Father's Day' presents, of course. I gave each of them a framed photo, my favorite of that kid and me doing something special."

"What a great idea." I was thinking how increasingly precious that photo would become over time.

"Well, I just wanted to thank you. I wouldn't have got out of my funk enough to do this without Wilda's suggestion that we talk with you, and I'm really glad I acted like a Dad, instead of just a man-in-the-middle-of-a-divorce. I guess it reminded me I'm going to have to stay pro-active as a father, even when I'm not a husband anymore. I'd just been thinking it would be automatic, but how would a kid know that? You know?"

"Yes, I do know," I replied. "I hope that more and more divorcing dads and moms can step up to take care of their kids' needs like you just did, Lyle."

"Thanks, Monza. My kids and I are really grateful. It was a good day for us."

When Laura called, my first thought was that I wondered how their kids had responded to both parents wanting to have a real "heart-to-heart" with them. And that's the first thing she said.

"Monza, I wanted you to know that the kids thought it was so cool that both their dad and I wanted to have a special ceremony just for them. I know this is tacky of me to say, but I couldn't believe it that Lyle got it together to do something like get those great pictures framed. Anyway, they were 'up for' whatever I had to say to them because Lyle's conversation with them had them 'primed.' It was great. When I talked to them and then they talked to me, it was all respectful and kind of solemn, compared to our usual way of bantering with each other. Then, when I gave them my gifts, they all came over and hugged and kissed me, one after another."

I had to ask: "Do you mind my asking what you gave them? I'm always curious what parents choose."

"Oh, no, I'm delighted to tell you. I had a bronze medallion made for each of them, with the gold key to our house set into it, and on the back it says, 'You always have the key to my heart and home. Mama.' I told them that they can choose whether to have it made into a pendant, pin, or a necklace. I'm so curious to see what each decides. Of course, they can change it later if they want. They seemed to like them a lot."

"I'm sure they do, Laura." I continued, "I know that as I grew older and my parents lived in different states, it always felt very grounding that I had a key to each of their homes. Made me feel that, no matter where I went as a young adult,

I had a home with both of my folks."

"Yes, that's what I want for Brian, Katie, and Jessica, so much I could cry." She laughed, "But I'm not in the mood for crying now. The 'divorce ritual' with our kids was one of the best times we've had with them since this whole process began. Thank you, Monza, for your help. I think the kids feel like they have two parents who are there for them, whatever changes are happening."

Guidelines for Parents' Separate Rituals with Children

1. Be careful not to assume that your partner would be unwilling to do her/his own ritual with the children. We know our partner in the context of an evolving relationship. When that relationship breaks down, we make faulty assumptions about what he/she is or isn't capable of doing, given that the person is functioning outside the relationship. Or, even if the person isn't initially inclined, he/she might make the choice to do, sensing that it might set the tone for her/his future relationship with the children.

   If Laura had told her attorney not to bother suggesting a ritual to Lyle, it might have altered the course of his relationship with his children.

2. A ritual can be as simple as what you would want to say to your children if you plan it out carefully. Be sure it includes the elements that let the children know about aspects of their future.

3. Think about what you want to say over time and keep a little notebook to jot down notes. It's hard to remember everything you'd like to include at once, so keeping a notebook can help you develop your ideas and then later organize the topics in the order that makes most sense to you. Some topics might be:

   a. What will be changing?

   b. What will be the same?

   c. How you feel about them?

   d. How you are going to treat their other parent?

4. Make your commitments clear about how you will be there for them, making sure what you say is realistic. You can address issues such as:

   a. How often they will be with you

   b. How you will treat their other parent

   c. How you intend to avoid saying negative things about the other parent (be realistic, e.g., "I might slip up sometimes.")

   d. How many school functions and other activities of theirs you will attend

   e. How you will support them financially, if appropriate, for college, sports

   f. Whether you will take them on vacations

5. Anticipate some of the issues that may make the child feel insecure so you can set them as ease, such as:

   a. Any fear they might have about whether you'll ever stop loving them as you did their mom or dad.

   b. Any issue there might be about whether you'll keep seeing them

6. For a ritual that is primarily a conversation, if possible, pick a place that is special to you and the kids, one that fosters a feeling of being in your own world together for a little bit

   a. Remember the guideline from Chapter 1, which is to avoid picking a restaurant or some other very public place. Instead, it can be:

    i. A place in nature where you've been together, of which you have good memories: mountains, a beach, park, or campground

    ii. A place of worship if it is special to all of you

    iii. At home. In this case, it is important to make the space special in some way, perhaps with flowers, and/or snacks that are special to the kids, perhaps with photos out of the family, or candles lit.

b. Avoid doing the ritual in a place that will prompt memories of arguments and battles, unless you make part of the ritual focus on letting go of past conflicts that happened there.

This letting-go process can be valuable if it is where the parent and children will still be living, but might be better performed as a separate ritual at another time, so you don't spread your focus too thin.

CHAPTER 3

Hostile Divorce: Parents Meet with Therapist and Attorneys to Make Basic Commitments in Front of Children

Forest and Evelyn   *Elana, 18*   *Myra, 14*

*E*lana, a student of mine at the university, came to my office to talk with me about an overdue paper. Her hands were shaking, and her eyelids were red. It wasn't long into our conference before she told me what was *really* bothering her.

"My mother," she said, "is calling me every night, taking me into her confidence about stuff I shouldn't even *know*! About my father's indiscretions, her fears about getting old, of being alone. See, they're getting a divorce, and it's super nasty. Their drama goes on and on and on. She blames him for *everything* that's wrong in her life! I can't sleep and I'm getting behind in all my classes! Besides, I'm worried sick about my little sister. She's only 14 and even though our nanny is trying to comfort her as much as she can, Myra keeps hearing the horrible arguments our parents are having, not to mention all the stuff from both our parents that she *really* shouldn't know.   My father's living in an apartment now, but still he calls Myra every night to make sure she's 'hearing both sides.'   And she told me our mother goes on rants at the dinner table whenever she happens to be home when he calls.   It's hell for Myra."

I asked, "Do you want to tell me about your folks? What's going on?"

Elana reported: Forest and Evelyn, her parents, were known as a "turbo-couple," both of them high-powered executives in Fortune 500 companies.   Frequently seen in newspaper society pages, well known in philanthropic circles, favorites at the country club, and members of several prestigious boards of trustees, these two were constantly on the go. The children had been raised primarily by nannies and private-school teachers.   The family was "picture perfect" on the outside, but profoundly shaky at the core.   While Forest's and Evelyn's marriage floundered, fueled by a common spitfire anger over petty differences and constant alcohol consumption whenever they were together, it was also failing, at a deeper level, due to harsh perfectionism on both their parts. Predictably, each blamed the other for the failure of the marriage.   Used to having their way, neither would give an inch from his or her position.   Their lawyers had made a bundle handling their divorce.

After listening to Elana for awhile, noticing that her

hands were *always* moving, I recommended that she make an appointment with a therapist I trust deeply, and she said she would. We didn't speak of it again, but I noticed that within a few weeks, Elana looked a little less haggard, and her work in class was satisfactory, if not always exactly on time.

A month later, Elana stopped by again during my office hours. Extremely bright but insecure, she fidgeted as she caught me up on what was going on. As so many 18-year-olds are wont to do, she had gotten herself into a last-minute crunch: she had a paper due the next day, and hadn't selected a topic. We discussed her options, given what most interested her in our readings, and soon she had a paper topic she could handle overnight. Then I asked, "How are you doing regarding your family at home, Elana?"

"Well, I *love* Dr. Rosen! She's as cool as you said, so smart and she really seems to care. My sessions with her are totally the best time of the week for me."

"I'm so happy it's a good match. I think the world of her."

"She's asked me to consider requesting a meeting with my whole family at her office. I want to know what you think of that idea. See, she thinks that Myra and I have a right to not be so caught in the middle between them, which sounds great to me, but I don't know if it could work or would just be asking for World War III. I'm really scared."

"I'm sure it *is* frightening! My parents weren't as explosive as you've described your parents to be, but I know a little about what you mean because I asked my mom to come to therapy during a crisis in our relationship. It was very scary ... but I believe I have a good relationship with my mother *now* because of the work we did together then."

"That's cool," Elana said. "OK, but I just don't know how to arrange it all ... I guess I could just ask 'em."

"Well," I thought a moment, "you might ask Dr. Rosen if she thinks there'd be any benefit in having your folks talk with her alone first so that she could prep them for the family meeting. Or, I'll ask her, since we're friends. Would you like me to do that?"

"Would you? I just think if my parents walked in cold turkey when they've only been talking through their lawyers, Myra and I would end up huddled in the corner under Dr. Rosen's desk while they throw things at each other!"

Aviva Rosen and I had our phone conversation about Elana's situation. I told her Elana's fear for her sister and herself in a family meeting, given the volatility of her folks. I said I thought that if she *could* get Elana's parents to come in alone to be told what their daughter needed before the family meeting, the young woman *might* feel more protected. Aviva said she knew one of the attorneys on their case, so she might call him to get his "take" on how much capacity they actually had to focus on their children, at least for a session. We agreed to stay in touch. She got Elana's permission to give general information to the attorney about how torn apart both girls were feeling about being caught in their parents' conflict.

As it turned out, the husband's attorney discussed the situation with the wife's attorney, and then the attorneys talked to their respective clients: they told them that Dr. Rosen, Elana's therapist, wanted to talk to them regarding a matter of importance regarding Elana and Myra. They encouraged their clients to meet with her. Ultimately, Forest and Evelyn and both of their attorneys met with Aviva to discuss what the two parents could do to help their children heal from their divorce. Aviva and both attorneys, well aware of the level of open conflict, were frank about the effect Forest and Evelyn's badmouthing each other was having on their girls, and how each parent was doing things that were hurting their children. Sitting in opposite corners of the room and never looking at each other, the two parents listened while the professionals told them about the power they'd seen in divorced parents' stating their intentions for making sure that they don't continue to involve their children in their conflict so that the kids wouldn't suffer any more than they already had. Forest and Evelyn, each looking rigidly sullen, occasionally exhaled audibly, nodded almost imperceptibly, and took notes, then agreed to a family meeting.

One afternoon not long after, this family met in Dr. Rosen's office, with both attorneys present as witnesses. It was not a long meeting. Dr. Rosen thanked everyone for being there, and said that she and Mr. Jensen, Evelyn's attorney, and Ms. Holberg, Forest's attorney, were there as witnesses. Then she turned it over to the parents.

Forest began talking to Elana and Myra, "We're having this meeting so that you girls can see each of us make a statement of our intentions. We're united in this one thing at least: We don't want to hurt you more than we already have. We each have something to say:

> For my part, I won't badmouth your mother. I may not always be perfect, but I'll really work at it. I won't try to get you to side with me against her. I won't try to drag you into our arguments or say sarcastic things about your mother when I have time with you. I will try my best to be civil about your mother when I'm with either of you girls. When all four of us are together, I'll be respectful of you and your mother so that I don't take anything **away** from celebrations that are special to you. Before these witnesses, these are my intentions."

Then Evelyn spoke, looking at her daughters with tears in her eyes: "I'm sorry that we've already hurt both of you as much as we have, my darlings. Before these witnesses I want to say:

> I won't badmouth your father. I won't try to get you to side with me against him. Elana, I won't use you as my confidante; I realize that hasn't been fair to you. I won't

act rejecting or harsh if you mention anything nice about your father, when you come home from some occasion with your dad, as I have with you, Myra. I won't act like a victim instead of a responsible mother. And when big occasions come for either of you, I want you to know that I'm going to try really hard to put your happiness before my feelings toward your father: I'll act appropriate, civil, and pleasant so that you can fully enjoy your special days without fear there's going to be another blow-up."

Aviva Rosen called me that night: "I didn't know they had it in 'em! It was short and sweet, but they really had done their homework, and their statements hit the mark. I really, really hope they'll keep their word. If they do, it will help both Elana *and* Myra tremendously."

One final note: Three years later, I was delighted to be invited to Elana's graduation party. It gave me special joy to see both of her parents hosting the party graciously, hugging her and her younger sister frequently, and clearly enjoying the festivities.

Variation on This Basic Ritual of Stating Intentions

The format of stating intentions can be used in many situations, by an individual or couple at the end of "closure counseling," or, in fact, years after a divorce or break-up is finalized. Over the years, I've found that many people— straight and gay, newly separated or long estranged—come to a deeper healing through simply writing out and speaking aloud a statement that can be as simple as the "speeches" Forest and Evelyn made to their daughters. In other situations, people choose to make their statements more fully, including the following elements:

1) what they still value about their former spouse or partner,

2) what they're glad to be "done with,"

3) what they regret or feel remorse about having done or not done,

4) what they intend to do/not do in any future relationship for their greater health.

Many times I have worked with therapists, members of the clergy, teachers, and attorneys to create outlines for such written or spoken statements. I am gratified whenever I hear of another person taking up the challenge of telling their whole truth in times of painful, yet growthful transition, thus empowering themselves to move forward in integrity and accountability.

Guidelines for Creating This "Ritual" of Stating Intentions

1. One of the children can initiate the request for a ritual statement of intentions on the part of one or both parents.

2. When needed, one of the children or a spouse can utilize the resources of professionals in the community-therapists, mediators, coaches, and attorneys-to help facilitate a meeting where the parents can make commitments to leave the children out of their battles.

   a. More and more professionals are working collaboratively to help families get through divorces by creating healthy transitions. As I mentioned in the introduction, movement has been initiated and forwarded by the International Academy of Collaborative Professionals, all professionals who work in the field of family law.

   b. Even attorneys who litigate and are representing opposing parties in a divorce, such as in Evelyn and Forest's case, can be a support for helping the parents make commitments that involve the health and well-being of their children

3. Having attorneys, a family friend, or clergy, as well as a therapist or other person familiar with the process of stating such intentions can provide a security net for the children when parents who are severely alienated come together to make known their intentions to support of their children's well-being.

It is important not to be intimidated by having more

people present during this process. In this case, having each parent's attorney, as well as the therapist, acted as a strong force in holding a container for the parents to act in integrity.

4. Such a meeting can be short and to the point. There is no need to try to make pleasant talk. In fact, it can backfire. A ritual statement of intentions can be just that-a clear statement followed by a conclusion of the meeting. Consider including the following elements:

   a. What will be the same

   b. How you feel about them

   c. How you are going to treat their other parent

   d. Making your commitments clear. Make sure what you say is realistic. You can address issues such as:

      i. How often you will be seeing the children

      ii. How you will treat their other parent

      iii. Not saying a lot of negative things about the other parent (be realistic, e.g., "I might slip up some-times.")

      iv. How many school functions and other activities you will attend

      v. How you will support the children financially, if appropriate, for college, sports, etc.

      vi. Whether you will take them on vacations

Be careful not to assume that your partner would be unwilling to do a ritual—either with you or separately.

CHAPTER 4

Abusive, Alcoholic Parent and Passive Parent: A Ritual with Support Group and Discussion with Sons

Eric and Janet   Marshall, 14   Ian, 12

*I*n some families, the focus may need to be on how one adult will commit to protecting the children from any ongoing conflicts with the other parent. If the parent is in need of support, it can be important to do a closure ritual with her/his own support group *before* he or she feels able to do a ritual with the children.

Janet B. called me at the suggestion of her pastor. He knew me from community work we had shared and had told her that he believed what I would offer could meet her needs better than he could. She said, "Pastor Sorensen believes what I've told him, but Eric, my soon-to-be-ex-husband, is also a parishioner of his. Eric is a pillar of the community, but—you've probably heard this before— he's also an alcoholic, abusive asshole … as well as the father of my two sons. I hate him, I absolutely hate him. But I don't want my boys to despise their father. I know I've got to do something about this hate that's eating me up before it poisons my kids, but I don't have a clue about what to do."

I told Janet I thought her goal was worthy and I'd be honored to look with her at possibilities for healing this hurt, and we set a time to meet.

At our initial meeting I asked her to tell me the story of her relationship with Eric, and she told the all-too-common tale: meeting in college, whirlwind courtship, unplanned pregnancy, and rushed marriage; two babies in three years, and 14 years of growing apart, growing frustration, and his rising anger and alcohol-fueled abuse of her, mostly emotional but sometimes physical as well. She said she'd been to the emergency room four times in 14 years, but added, "You are the first person I have told that those four trips were not because of household accidents."

I was aware that her report focused almost solely on Eric's part in "ruining the marriage," so I asked the tough question that I believe is always crucial for healing to begin: "Janet, what do you think your part was in bringing you to this point?" I have found that a person's response to this question says a great deal about her/his consciousness.

After tearfully staring out the window for a few moments, Janet whispered, "I gave up on myself. I just gave up my *self*. I got passive in every area of our life except in the care of my children. And the weaker and more passive I got, the more domineering Eric got. And the more demanding he got, the more servile I got until finally I was his slave much more than his wife. For several years, I believed he liked it better that way, and was nicer to me than he would have been if I'd challenged him, so I convinced myself it was right. But the fourth time he beat me up bad enough for me to have to go to emergency, something finally clicked. I heard inside my head, 'Janet Lynn, you are as sick as he says you are if you continue to allow him to hurt you—and I didn't raise you to live like this.' I believe it was my father's voice. He died in a logging accident when I was 13. I know it was him because he was the one who never let me allow my brothers to win just because they were boys; he was the one who'd told me I could go to college if I wanted to; he was the one who said, 'No man worth his salt ever raises a hand to a woman.'

"So the next morning before I got released from the hospital, I called a divorce attorney. Then I called Eric at work and told him to go home, pack his clothes and check into a motel so he wouldn't be there when I got home. I haven't looked back, even when he calls and begs me to reconsider 'for the sake of the boys.' The divorce'll be final in two weeks. Funny thing is, after all his years of bullying, he hasn't fought me on one single point about the divorce. I bet he knows my attorney knows all about his 'dirty laundry,' so he'd better keep his mouth shut. He's just terrified that if his 'secret' starts getting out, it will ruin his public reputation, I'm sure.

Whatever else he is, he's not dumb."

I asked her how her sons, Marshall and Ian, ages 14 and 12, were doing. She replied, "They don't say much, but they hug me a lot, and they are always sneaking peeks, checking out whether my face looks like I've been crying or not. They do say they like how peaceful it is at home now. And they don't want to go out with their dad most of the time when he calls to take them to a ball game or out to dinner. It's clear they're mad at him; most of the time when they get off the phone, one will say, 'He's a jerk,' and the other will answer, 'Yeah, A-1.' I don't talk about my feelings at all because I'm so angry I'm afraid I'll make them hate him as much as I do. But then I worry that I'm just being passive again, withholding vital information they should have as they grow into men."

"Who do you talk to? Who are your allies?" I asked.

"I'm in a support group with five other women. We all had kids the same age. Over the years we started meeting every week, first just for coffee, and then gradually we started telling each other the nitty-gritty about our lives. I talk to them, but you know, until I filed for divorce, I'd never told them about Eric's alcoholism and abuse. I guess I thought it was disloyal or something. And also I was so embarrassed to be such a wimp. So retro, you know."

"I think that's very common," I reflected back. "If you decide that you'd like to create a ritual of reclaiming your life as a strong single woman, perhaps you would like to invite your support group to share it with you."

"Yes! They *would* be the people who would understand. To tell you the truth, I think there are a couple of them who are thinking about doing the same thing."

I told Janet my theory of the power of ritual to cement our intentions within our minds, hearts, and even bodies. I shared my thoughts about how rituals could be more or less formal.

She said, "I want you to be there. It was very important to me when I was married that a minister married us. And I want a minister to 'un-marry' me. And I do want my support group to witness this! What else I want isn't so clear."

I suggested that she make a list of things she wanted to release, never to repeat, completely let go of. I also asked her to consider making a list of things for which she thanked Eric, especially her sons, but also any other good things she had received from him. Finally I told her how valuable I had seen it be for others to state intentions of what she wanted in her life, her "Want Ad to the Universe." She agreed to work on all those lists.

When Janet invited her support group to her Divorce Ritual, every one of the women in her group, exclaimed, "What a brilliant idea!" They suggested that they would each bring her a gift that symbolized a quality that they wished for her to have either in greater abundance or for the first time in her adult life. And they offered to provide the meeting space and refreshments.

Janet chose the night of the Friday she signed the divorce papers for her ritual. Marshall and Ian had left on a weekend trip with another family who had two boys their ages, so she knew she would have the entire weekend alone to assimilate all of the insights the ritual might bring her. She asked me to be the "MC" ("Mistress of Ceremony") for the ritual, to bless this special gathering. She made it clear that she wanted it to be a "spiritual" event, and that she wanted me to use whatever "spiritual" language I would comfortably use.

When I arrived, the living room in which we were meeting was full of candlelight, the floor was covered with comfortable pillows as well as sofas and reading chairs. Janet introduced me to each woman in her support group. They were all eager to begin.

As Janet and I had agreed, I opened the circle by saying, "Dearly beloved, we are gathered together here tonight to honor the Dissolution of the Marriage of Janet and Eric, to release her from the vows she made to him, to affirm what she learned and received from her marriage, to bear witness to her intentions for moving forward in her life after the divorce that has just been made final, and to offer her our gifts, our blessings for her journey that begins tonight. May we all give and receive what we need the most from this sharing."

Janet thanked all of us for being with her on this night.

She said, "It means the world to me to have you each as a friend. I want to tell you all the things I've been listing in private at Monza's suggestion. I hope that by saying them out loud, I will not only take them into myself more deeply, but that I'll also let you know me better, which I believe is important to my healing from the secrets I have surrounded myself with for fifteen years."

She shared first her list of what she wanted to let go of, to release: her burning anger at Eric for all the cruel things he had done to her, said to and about her; her hatred of herself for putting up with his abuse for so long; her belief that she deserved what she got. She spoke about her shame and sorrow over what had become of the coed at the university who had dreams of making a positive difference in the world, the young woman who had healthy self-esteem before she let Eric damage it. She said she wanted her heart to be free of hate.

We responded as a group, "May it be so."

She followed that list by naming the gifts she acknowledged receiving from Eric: Marshall and Ian; a beautiful house and enough money to give the boys music lessons and sports camps and other positive experiences for their development; financial security that would enable her sons to go to college without going into crippling debt; the intelligence and sense of humor he had shared with his sons, etc. The list, although small, was significant.

At my suggestion, the group repeated in unison, "May

we all be truly grateful for these gifts you have received."

Finally, Janet avowed her intention to be kind to herself and expect any other human being she was close to from this day forward to be kind to her; to reclaim her self-esteem by learning and practicing what she was good at; to be open to love, not close off in fear that no one could be different from Eric; to be a good model of a strong, loving and self-loving woman for her sons so that they would be more respectful of women than their father and not compare themselves with their father at all; and to discover freedom and laughter and playfulness again.   There were other things on her list, but this gives the idea.

As her witnesses, we responded, "May it be so."

During the next part of the ritual, each member of her support group gave her a gift that symbolized a blessing she wished for Janet (this idea appears in Kris Radish's novel *Dancing Naked at the Edge of Dawn,* in which friends hold a "Reverse Bridal Shower" for the protagonist).   When one woman gave her a sculpture of a dancing child, she said, "I want for you to be able to reclaim your childlike spirit of complete freedom to dance whenever and wherever and with whomever you wish."   Another told a story of a time Janet had brought a ray of light to one of her hardest times, when she felt like she was in a fog she couldn't escape from, thanked her, wished her plenty of light and clarity to help her through whatever might yet come, and gave her a pair of candlesticks, both of which were shaped like a woman with her arms outstretched with a set of six candles of various colors. Still another handed Janet a basket full of luxurious bath products with an envelope that held a gift certificate for a massage and said, "I hope with all my might that you will pamper yourself as the beautiful, miraculous woman that you are, and that with this massage your body will heal from whatever hurts it has borne." The gifts and the blessings were as varied as the women in the circle, and all of them were perfect for Janet. Tears and laughter came in waves, and I watched as this group bonded deeply, focusing on Janet *and* learning new facets of each other as they spoke and listened.

I asked Janet and each of her friends to pray or meditate in whatever way felt true for each of them. Then, after a few moments of silence, I knelt before Janet, placed my hands on her head, and pronounced, "By the power vested in me as a minister, and with deep trust in your ability to be whole and free, I now pronounce you released from the vows you made on June 20, 1978, to Eric B. May you feel the blessing of the Divine and all of us as you move forward from this day of Divorce, your day of reclamation of your personal independence. In your newfound autonomy, may you feel accompanied each day and night for the rest of your life by the intimacy of this sacred circle, by the wisdom you have gained from your own experience and the offerings of your friends, the insights you have garnered from this ritual, and by the presence of the One who has made you and knows you by name."

And then the party began! As women brought food and wine out of the kitchen, and the music came forth from the sound system, Janet and her support group eased into playful, loving banter. They looked at all the gifts carefully, and commented on how right each was. And Janet glowed from the inside out. When I left after an hour, the celebration was still going strong.

Guidelines for a Divorce Ritual with a Group of Friends

1. Create a ritual that provides the kind of framework and focus that will meet your needs rather than trying to accommodate group members.

   a. You may want something more secular, more spiritual in a wider sense of the word, or in keeping with the tenants of a particular religion.

   b. While honoring the kind of framework you need, make sure you are comfortable using it in the group of friends you have chosen.

      i. This may vary widely depending on the how reserved or open you are, as well as other influences, such as gender, sexual orientation, level of intimacy with the friends, similarities or differences in beliefs, etc.

      ii. If you realize you would not be comfortable in the group with the framework you want for the ritual, you may want to:

      • adapt the framework slightly,

      • select a different group,

      • invite fewer people for the ritual, including just those you'd be utterly comfortable with.

2. Tell the group in advance what the framework will be for the ritual, so if anyone is *not* comfortable, he or she has the option of deciding not to participate. Even in an ongoing support group, some people simply need not to participate in a certain event and should be welcome to decline.

Whatever your own framework is, create the ritual so that no group member has to actively participate in a part of the ritual that might violate her or his own beliefs.

Find out ahead of time what you need to know about participants' comfort level with what you intend to do. Assume that you may need to explain or educate your group of friends about how you understand the purpose of the ritual, given that such ceremonies are new for many people.

3. Create an atmosphere where disparaging comments about your ex are not made, for the most part, including humorous ones, as it can inadvertently hold you (and your support group) in the mind-set of past hurt and anger, as well as perpetuating an adversarial dynamic between you and your ex-spouse.

   a. Keep the focus on your own freedom and power to be who you want to be as you move forward in your own life.

   b. Endeavor to imagine this ritual as an opportunity for all who participate to stretch and grow, to heal themselves, not just as a gift you alone are receiving.

Conveying the Ritual to Children Who Were Not Present

Someone who chooses to mark this passage with friends has several directions she/he can move from this point. Sometimes, that ritual is all a person wants or feels is needed. For some others, however, the need to do *something* with the children still feels important, even if it is not a formal ritual. Some people choose to speak to each child individually, tailor-making the conversation to the child's age and capacity for processing. Others choose to have a dinner table conversation about some basic changes they may want to make in attitudes, handling conflicts, house rules, setting up family meeting times for sharing current issues, etc. Still others simply ask the children if they have any questions or concerns that need attention, and then address those particular issues, letting the children dictate what gets dealt with according to their own timing. A parent could also have a completely separate ritual with the children, as Lyle and Laura each did in Chapter Two.

Janet's Process with Marshall and Ian

In Janet's situation, her son Marshall created the opening for further processing of the major change in their lives. When the boys got home after their weekend away, they were full of news and, of course, hungry. So the three of them prepared dinner, and as they ate, Marshall and Ian told Janet about the fun they'd had with their friends at an amusement park, a video arcade, riding dune buggies, and playing a hundred different card games. Janet said, "I'm so glad you guys had fun! That really makes me happy!"

"So, Mom," Marshall asked, "were you happy having a weekend to yourself? What'd you do?"

Janet had wondered how she would bring up the subject of her Divorce Ritual, and now she smiled, realizing that her sensitive 14-year-old son opened the door for her. "I missed you, AND I had a wonderful weekend!" she replied. "I did a Divorce Ritual on Friday night with my support group, and I'll tell you about it if you want."

"Yeah, what's a Divorce Ritual anyway?" Ian chimed in.

"Well, there were things I needed to say about what I wanted to let go ..."

"Well, duh, like Dad!" Marshall rolled his eyes.

"Ha, ha, yeah, but more like feelings that I don't want to keep, such as feeling bad about myself for being so weak I let him hurt me ... and there were things I wanted to name that I thank him for ..."

"US!" Ian chortled and did a little dance movement behind his chair.

"Absolutely. You were at the top of the list. And our home. And Dad's making enough money so you can do all the things you like to do ... then I made some intentions about things I want to do and ways I want to be that are better for me than how I've been in the past."

"So, Mom, are you going to change a lot? I like how you

are, well, most of the time," Marshall said shyly.

"Don't worry, honey, I didn't have a lobotomy. I'm not going to be all that different to you guys! You still have to put your dirty clothes in the hamper and clean the kitchen after dinner."

"Aww ..." Ian whined.

"Seriously," Janet continued, "I want to be more respectful of myself, and I needed to say out loud what I want for the rest of my life, and my friends were really there for me. They even gave me presents to show what they want for me."

"Anything we'd like?" Ian looked hopeful.

"Naw, no video games, buddy. But they are beautiful to me. And I'll show them to you later if you're interested."

"Mom," Marshall said quietly, "I'm glad you did something like that ... ritual thing ... for yourself. Ian and I, we talked about you and Dad getting a divorce while we were gone, and ... we're glad you're not with Dad anymore. We kind of wish we could get a divorce from him, too."

"What do you mean, honey?" Janet knew she needed to be very careful at this point, not to jump on an "'anti-Eric bandwagon."

"Well, you know, it's not like we haven't seen how mean he was, how he treated you, talked to you, and," he hesitated, "hurt you. Also how he talks to us ..."

"'Lectures' us is more like it," Ian added.

"Yeah, he always has to be the 'big man,'" Marshall went on. "Plus, you know, he's really nasty when he drinks.

Sometimes he calls us, and he's almost drunk, all loud and bossy and then acts like we must be missing him ... Mom, it's really lame. Please don't ever make us live with him, OK?"

"Were you worried that I would?" Janet asked.

"Well, when Mr. and Mrs. McGovern got divorced, the boys went with their dad and the girls stayed with their mom."

"I don't think our situation is the same, guys, but I understand that you might worry about a lot of things. What might change. What might be hard. What I want you to know is that both your dad and I agree we want your lives to be as consistent and good as possible. Your dad hasn't ever been a 'hands-on' kind of father because of his work, mostly, but also probably because of his personality. So, from my point of view, it makes the most sense that I'll keep on being the primary caregiver until you become independent. Unless you don't agree and then we could certainly discuss it more if you wanted to."

"Are you counting the days until then?" Marshall asked.

"Not in the least, honey! At least not when you're not being a brat! Ha, ha. Are you worried that I don't want to be a mom anymore since I am not a wife anymore?"

"Well, I guess I wondered if you'd get 'anti-male' on us."

"Ahh. No, my anger at your father is only at him. It doesn't spill over on you. It's not that he's a man that caused our problems, it's choices that he made as a person. You have the ability to make better choices, and that's what I want you guys to remember."

"Okaaaayyyyy," Ian said as if he were being put-upon, to signal his being "done" with this serious conversation. "What's for dessert?"

"One last thing," Janet said, "and then dessert. I really want each of you to know that we can talk about anything about this divorce business as it comes along. We'll make our way through working things out with Dad together. And I want to hear any worry or question or hurt that you have. Please don't keep them locked down or feel like you have to just talk to each other. I can handle your feelings as well as my own. The end."

"Thanks, Mom," Marshall said. "Yeah, thanks, Mom," added Ian. And then they raided the freezer for ice cream to go with their favorite chocolate-chip cookies Janet had bought especially for their homecoming.

Later, when Janet went to check on the boys after they had gone to bed, Ian whispered, "Mom, come here a minute—I wanna tell you something."

"Sure, honey," Janet whispered back, "what's up?"

"Mom, I don't really want Marsh to know this, but I don't really want to go on any more overnights for awhile, OK?"

"Ian, it's OK, and I'd like to know why, if you'd be willing to tell me."

"Well … I just don't like to be away from you so soon after Dad's gone." He was fighting back tears. "I got scared that both of you would be gone when we got back. Kinda dorky, prob'ly, but I freaked out."

"Ian, I understand completely. I'm not going anywhere, honey. But I can certainly respect your feelings about not wanting to go away from home in these next few weeks or months."

"OK, thanks, Mom. Don't tell Marsh, OK?"

"I won't say a word, Ian. But maybe you'll tell him yourself in time."

As she walked toward her bedroom, Janet thought, "So much for Marshall being 'the sensitive one'."

Guidelines Regarding Process with Children Outside of the Ritual

1. Notice consciously when children take the lead and create the timing for the kind of informal conversation that can have the healing power of ritual. Take that opportunity in the moment, rather than waiting.

   The *exception* to this is if you are afraid, at that moment, that your own feelings will be too raw, or you can't control your own hurt or anger.

2. Be honest about any issues the children have witnessed or can understand.

   a. Recognize the issue, without rehashing it from a place of any of your own bitterness and hurt.

   b. It's vital that children not be made to suffer from denying any reality you all lived with.

   c. Don't dwell too much on the details, unless the children have questions and/or need to process their own feelings in more depth.

   Note: If the questions one child has are not appropriate for the age-level and understanding (or any other reason) of another child, ask to continue that conversation later; then be sure to do so.

3. Make sure that the children don't equate hurtful behavior on the part of either your ex or you with gender (Janet's husband hit her. He is a man. She didn't hit him. She is a woman. The boys are both male. Ergo. Men hit women).

Even if children don't discuss whether they see certain behaviors as gender-based, they may still draw these conclusions in their mind, so it's good to ask about it, for example: "Do you think that dad hit me because he's a man? Or because he was alcoholic? Or for some other reason?"

4. Discuss abusive behavior or attitudes in terms of individual choice or in the context of the psychology of the dynamic so it can become a life-lesson (without the lecture) that equips children to understand that they can make more constructive choices.

- For example: Janet might have said, "I don't know if your father would have been as angry or hit me if he hadn't become alcoholic. I do know that any tendencies he had were made far worse by his drinking."

- Or she could say: "I think your dad is one of the people who tries to get his power by giving orders to others. I think there are ways to be wise and strong and respected without giving orders."

CHAPTER 5

A Step-Parent Creates a Ritual for a Teenage Son

Frank and Pam Matt, 16

I have seen many children and teens suffer when they have virtually grown up with a step-parent or a parent's partner, only to have that person unceremoniously yanked from their lives when a divorce or break-up occurs. They often ask, "Will I ever see her/him again? Did she/he ever really care about me, or was it 'an act'? Does she/he still think about me at all, or am I just 'poof' gone from her/his mind? Why didn't she/he even say goodbye to me?" At times, this "unofficial" parent has been central to the child's security or sense of self, and when it's suddenly "over," just because the child's legal parent is no longer with the step-parent or partner, it can be frightening and/or emotionally damaging for the child/teen.

In cases such as these, having a private ritual with the

child/teenager is often a profound gift, reassuring and affirming of the particular bond that has been created.

Frank phoned me on a Friday, saying his therapist had recommended he call. He said he was in the midst of a "nasty divorce" (his words) and he felt the need to mark his ongoing commitment to his step-son, who was like his own kid.

"What exactly are you feeling a need for with your son?"

He paused for a moment, then replied, "Matt lives part of the time with his mother, part of the time with me. I'm glad she felt, even after we split, it was important for him to have a male role-model during these years, and I'm also happy to give her a little 'time-off.' I know it's a tough job alone. Now I feel the need to do more somehow than just talk with him over pizza or a game of golf about my 'take' on things. I want him to have some 'symbol,' you might say, to hold onto so he still knows believes that I want to be a dad to him.

"I think you're wise. And I want to also say that if he, as you said, 'is like a son' to you, then he is your son by choice, in your heart. I hope you'll keep hold of that clearly in your own mind, instead of feeling insecure. It will help Matt to feel secure in your love."

Frank let out a long breath. "Wow. Yeah. I need to remember that part about my own security as a dad. He really *is* my only child."

We talked more about the ritual. Frank said, "I don't

want to badmouth his mother; I just want to speak for myself. I want to do whatever I can to help him feel secure with me. And I think Matt would take it in more deeply somehow if I state my absolute commitment to him in a serious, maybe 'ceremonial' way. He's 16, and quite mature in some ways, but I'm sure this whole process has shaken him to his core. Matt isn't very forthcoming about his feelings, but I know he feels things deeply. He's actually quite a lot like me."

I told Frank I'd be happy to co-create a ritual with him, whether he wanted to do it alone with Matt or with a witness present, be it his therapist or me. We set a time to meet the next Wednesday.

Frank shared that he and his therapist had talked at length about the need for him to create an autonomous relationship with Matt before he finished high school and went off to college so their bond would stay intact.

"I want," he said, "to make some vows to Matt. I want him to know he's my 'forever family,' that as far as I'm concerned there are some facts about who we are to each other that are not up for negotiation. But I don't know how formal I should be? How can I frame it so it will feel significant, but not freak him out?"

I replied, "I believe that the ritual or ceremony itself need not be formal for the words to hold great significance. I also think that being honest with Matt about your intentions is vital; he's old enough to see through any falseness, so your credibility is on the line. If you want him to take this seriously, he deserves to know why it feels so serious to you." I continued, "I also would suggest that you think about some gift you want to give him that would be a symbol of what you want to say. My experience is that, even if kids forget every word a parent says during a ritual, they remember the significance of the event every time they look at, feel, or use that symbol. It might be a key to your house, jewelry, or a framed photo of the two of you. Those are just ideas. You know what's right for you and Matt."

He said, "Matt'll probably feel more comfortable if I do this alone with him, but would you look over what I write out to say, give me feedback on it? It feels like I've got this one chance, and if I blow it, I'll regret it big time."

"I know what you mean, Frank," I responded, "but I believe that whatever you say that is honest and heartfelt will resonate with him. And yes, I'll be happy to help in any way I can."

A few days later I got an e-mail in which Frank had written out his vows to Matt. They moved me to tears. I e-mailed him a response, asking him a few questions, including if I could use his vows as a sample in a book I hoped to write one day on this topic. He said he was happy to share anything that could make it easier for somebody else in this "god-awful mess you never imagine when you're getting married." Frank decided to give Matt a signet ring with his family crest on it, inlaid with his son's initials, to mark the occasion of their post-divorce vows. He said he'd decided to meet with Matt alone in a place special to them. I assured him I thought that was a great choice, given Matt's age, and told him I would be praying for them, that I'd love to hear how it went.

Frank's vows to Matt went like this:

I, Frank, promise you, Matt, that you are now and forever my family, my son. Wherever I am, you have a home. Matt, to the best of my ability, I will support you with my spiritual, mental, emotional, and financial resources so that you can get the educational and extra-curricular experiences (sports camps, trips abroad, etc.) that will help you to become the man you are meant to be. I trust that you will do your part, by working as a student and participant, and, as you are able, a worker, too. Once you are through college, my son, I expect you to make your own way; but I want for you to know that, until then, you do not have to worry about having your basic needs met. I make you that commitment.

I, Frank, promise to trust you, Matt, to tell me what you need, what you think, and what you dream. And you can trust that I will listen carefully, advise you if you ask for advice, and let you find your own way when you don't ask or don't choose to take my advice.

I, Frank, promise you, Matt, that I will continue to hold your mother in respect; you do not need to be afraid that I will try to pull your affections away from her because we are now divorcing. I truly want for you to feel the love of two parents. I pray that you will not feel torn between us; that is a tear I would never wish on you, and I will do everything in my power to do or say nothing that would cause you to feel a conflict of loyalties.

I, Frank, promise you, Matt, that you can tell me anything, ask me anything, call me anytime for any reason, night or day. I want you to know I love you unconditionally, my son. Whatever might be the worst thing you could ever do, I want you to know there will be someone willing to stay beside you, help you face its consequences like the man I know you are.

I hereby make these vows to you on the seventh day of March, 1998.

The second week of March Frank called me and said, "Not only was the experience of saying my vows to Matt terrific, but we also had an amazing talk afterward over pizza and root beer. He opened up about a lot of his feelings about the divorce, his mother *and* me, and he said that every vow I'd made addressed the things he'd been stewing over for months. He called me 'Dad' for the first time ever. I almost broke up completely. He said, 'I never knew you were a mind-reader.' I actually read it to him, carefully, making sure I had good eye contact. I wanted him to hear it in the best way I knew how to say it. Oh, and he loved the ring. He didn't say a lot about it, but he kept twisting it around and looking at it all through dinner. I feel great about having done this, Monza, I really do."

Guidelines for a Ritual shared by Step-Parent and a Child/ Teenager

1. A ritual can be created around a formal statement of commitment you want to make to your child to create trust and security for the future.

2. You can write out the words, just as you might write out words for a marriage commitment and then read them or memorize them.

3. You can make this commitment focusing only on your own intentions, without making reference to the other parent's behavior or your feelings regarding the other parent.

4. Your ritual does not have to include any expectation for the child/teen to participate or respond in any prescribed way.

   Your child might receive the commitment without sharing her/his own feelings, or, as Matt did, might open up about his/her own fears and feelings.

5. I don't advise ending this ritual (or any ritual) and then going separate ways immediately. Make a thoughtful transition back into "everyday" activity.

   a. At the end of the ritual, after the child/teen has had a chance to respond initially, provide some activity that shifts back to a more everyday interaction and still leaves time for the possibility of more conversation in a relaxed atmosphere if the child/teen seems inclined.

   b. Make sure that the transition time is truly relaxed, that

you don't get invested in asking questions about the ritual, saying anything "convincing" about how important
it was to do it, etc. Sometimes, a parent's tendency be
eager can be interpreted as pushy, and, for a teenager,
"pushy" is deadly.

CHAPTER 6

Divorcing Couple with Adopted Children Ritualize Their Commitment to Continue Co-Parenting

Fritz and Patrick   Nguyen, 10   Perry, 8

*A*mina, a new friend I'd met through a creative writing student of mine, asked me to come to an exhibit of her art. Before the show actually opened, she wanted me to help me write her artist's statement and give some titles to works she couldn't yet name. I found the prospect intriguing. Walking through her studio with her, getting a feeling of her work so that I could "speak her language" about her vision, I was struck by a portrait of a beautiful family: two dads and two children, a boy and a girl. I exclaimed, "What a gorgeous family! So full of light and happiness."

"They *are* stunning, aren't they?! Sad to say, they're splitting up." Amina walked right on, and I followed her, feeling a sad sigh fill me as I thought of parents making once again what might well be the best choice for themselves, yet upsetting little kids who didn't bargain for the chaos when they came into this family.

The night of the show's opening, I noticed the family from the portrait among the attendees, greeting Amina, and looking at their portrait on the wall with her other work. The children were clearly excited to be part of a professional exhibition. "Papa!" shouted the little girl, "we're famous!" and everyone surrounding them laughed delightedly. The two men smiled at her and each other.

At some point I was talking to Amina, and the family came near. "Patrick, Fritz, I want you to meet Monza, one admirer of your portrait!"

As we shook hands, I added, "Indeed I am! And from what I see tonight, Amina really captured your essences! I remember telling her when I first saw the portrait that I was struck by the light and happiness in each face. She really has a gift for capturing the spirit in people, doesn't she?" We all agreed about Amina's particular talent for tuning in to inner qualities every bit as much as outer details in all of her work—landscapes, still lives, or portraits. And then we all moved on as people do at such events.

Perhaps a month later I was in a café, reading a magazine and sipping my latté, when one of the men from that couple appeared. "Hi! I'm Patrick, would you mind if I sat down? There aren't any other chairs." I smiled, gestured for him to take a seat. "You're Monza, right?" I nodded. "My partner Fritz and I had dinner with Amina the other night and she told us a little more about you, more than just that you liked our picture. When we told her we really liked her artist's statement at the show, she gave you all the credit for it!"

"It was really fun," I answered truthfully. "She had all the pieces in her list of what she wanted to include, but I guess words are my medium instead of paint, so we just put our forces together! I love collaborating like that."

"Cool." There was a radiance in his smile, even brighter in person than on canvas. "She also said you combine your interest in creativity with spirituality. We were both very interested in that. Fritz went to seminary for awhile back in the 60s but he just couldn't figure out a way to be a gay priest, though the Episcopal Church, where he was raised, was already talking about it. He says he thinks he was just 'in the wrong place at the wrong time.'

"Anyway, after Amina told us about your work and the non-traditional rituals you do for times of transition, both of us thought it sounded very interesting, in a personal way, with our separation and wanting to continue to co-parent. Could we talk to you sometime about doing a ritual with our family?"

"I'd be more than delighted to do it."

"We'll call you soon," Patrick said, adding, "Great coincidence to run into you," he laughed, "or maybe more like serendipity."

When I met with Patrick and Fritz, they told me some history about their relationship and their adopted children. A few years before he and Patrick met, Fritz had adopted Nguyen as a way to fulfill a life-long wish to "be a better dad than [his] had been." Also, when he'd been in the army he'd made himself a promise to adopt a child from someplace torn up by war. While he'd had Nguyen for ten years, he and Patrick had been parenting her together for eight. Shortly after he and Patrick got together, they learned that a little guy at Nguyen's nursery school, Perry, aged two, was up for adoption because his foster mom had just been diagnosed with cancer, and his own mother and father had already had their parental rights terminated. Patrick had always wanted to parent, too, and they agreed that having a girl and a boy would be ideal for them and for the kids. They already knew and loved Perry, whom Nguyen adored. In fact, the two kids had already "chosen" each other, got along famously at school. So that's how their family had come together. "And now," Patrick said, "with two happy kids, ten and eight, our life has taken an unexpected turn."

At that point in the story Patrick looked at Fritz, and I got the idea that it was Fritz's call about how to tell whatever came next.

Fritz said, "Ah, I don't know exactly how to give you the brief version of our current situation ..."

"Just feel free to tell me whatever you want," I said. "I don't require a 'Reader's Digest' version."

Fritz told me that in the past year and a half he'd fallen deeply in love with a man named Jonah, a guy in his running club. He and Patrick had spent months talking about that "fact" before he ever acted on his feelings. Patrick thought it would feel OK to him for Fritz to have an affair as long as he always had safe sex and kept his commitments to him and the kids. So Fritz and Jonah had moved forward in their relationship, but after four months Patrick found that he couldn't handle the huge drain of Fritz's energy. Patrick said, "You know, I really was less concerned about his sleeping with Jonah than the fact that he was just 90% 'gone' from me in every way."

Nodding his head in agreement, Fritz continued to say that was when they began to talk about divorce. But they both completely broke up whenever they thought of separating Nguyen and Perry, and of the ramifications for the kids *and* themselves.

Moreover, they still really liked each other. They loved their own friendship, and the friendships they had made over the years with other people, and, most important, they really valued parenting together.

So they had started creating a plan by which Fritz and Jonah would live together. Patrick would live with the kids during the week, but they would have times that the kids would be with the two of them, their primary dads (like their usual Wednesday night Teriyaki Dinner and some time on Sunday). They also planned that the kids spend regular time with Fritz and Jonah (from Friday night to Sunday morning, except for one Friday night a month when the two primary dads would have social time with friends) so that Patrick could have two nights and one entire day off for himself, etc. They both said that figuring it all out equitably and thoughtfully had been the hardest and most valuable part of the whole process.

Patrick continued, "Our counselor helped us come to and articulate our top values: the need to have set specific times for certain activities and for those to be commitments we keep, no matter what, but also to stay flexible regarding school activities, sports events, etc.; trading holidays, again with flexibility whenever some particular extended-family event might require a change in our overall calendar; the need we both have for the kids to feel totally at home with both main dads, whether here or at Fritz and Jonah's; and our absolute value about keeping our conflict to ourselves (and our friendly neighborhood therapist), not fighting in front of the kids or badmouthing each other to the kids."

I asked a few questions (for instance, how Jonah dealt with their process *and* the kids; how were the kids doing with the "shifts'" they'd already experienced). After awhile, the conversation naturally turned to the anticipated ritual.

"What are your thoughts so far about what you'd like?" I asked.

"Well, we've come to the end of our actual divorce process and we've signed all of our agreements, done all the legal stuff necessary to protect the children and our primary assets as the parents of these kids, but we both feel something's missing on a spiritual level. We want to have a ceremony for the four of us, our primary family unit. But we don't even know how to talk with each other about what might be spiritual because we don't even use the same language."

I asked each of them how they envisioned their connection with a Divine or creative force, something within and/or beyond themselves, how they talked about that inside themselves when they felt solace, connection, or meaning. They did have very different words, but they were both clearly able to articulate their spiritual "universe." I suggested that from this conversation, they might see the points at which their understandings might meet, some language that might feel accurate and meaningful to both of them. Moreover, I asked them to consider that this process might offer them language that they could continue to use with their kids so that they'd have a consistent "spiritual vocabulary'" in their family.

Then I shared my vision of "ritual" and added, "Parents with children, like the two of you, can choose which regrets you want to share with the children, and which ones you want to share with each other alone."

We discussed how giving their children an appropriate symbol of their *commitment to continuity* would be especially imperative because their children had each already been separated from their birth parents. Now, having their adoptive parents split up could create even deeper levels of insecurity. I said, "If possible, choosing a gift that shows the love and closeness remaining even when there is separation will be crucial. I believe the two of you certainly have the will to make your kids' 'growing up family' as stable as you can make it."

At the end of our meeting, both Patrick and Fritz said they felt sure they could take it from there, and promised they'd tell me how it went.

A month later I got a beautiful card in the mail, which read, "Our Divorce Ritual was truly the highlight of our past year. Our kids chose to have it up in the hills at sunset, and all four of us spoke.

"We decided to give have lockets made for all four of us that looked like coins but open up and have a picture of our family inside. We gave them gold chains and told them they can wear the lockets, or keep them in a safe place, whatever works for them at different times in their life. And we bought four extras and said we'd keep them, so if any of us ever loses one, we'd have another one! It was symbolic of not having to be afraid to lose us. They loved them and insisted that we all put them on right that minute. We each helped put them on.

"Putting our commitment into words brought deep peace to us Dads, and we watched our kids shine in the security of what *is still true* in a way we haven't seen for months. Thank you for showing us the way. Fritz and Patrick."

Guidelines for This Ritual
to Affirm Continued Co-Parenting

1. If a divorcing couple has a child or children who have been adopted and/or have already been through one divorce/separation of parents, it is vital to take the impact of repeated separation into account during the ritual and/or in the selection of symbolic gifts.

2. If one partner is already involved with someone else, it is usually best to do a family ritual with only the original family, but in some cases, if everyone has accepted the new person, he or she could be included.

3. Make meticulous decisions about what "sorrows" to share with the children, and which to share alone with the other adult.

For other ideas, you may want to look at the guidelines in Chapters 7 and 8, which also focus on rituals shared with young children.

CHAPTER 7

Hostile Divorce: A Ritual for a Parent and Children after the Other Parent Has Left while the Children Are Away

Lila and Bob   *Mischa, 9*   *Kara, 6*

*O*ne day, a colleague at the university told me her sister was going through a rough patch in a complicated divorce. She said, "Last night we talked on the phone for three hours! She's absolutely devastated... not because of the divorce *per se,* but because of the impact it's having on her kids! Her ex just handed her the signed papers, told her he'd already packed his stuff, and he left for parts unknown while the kids were at camp. He told her, 'I'm not good with words, I have no idea what to say to them.' She said what I already knew: 'He's such a chicken-shit, he couldn't even hang around to say goodbye to his own kids.' Now the kids are saying, 'What's the deal? Do we have a dad or not? Did he divorce us as well as you? Will we ever see him again? Did he ever love us? Does he hate all of us so much he couldn't even say goodbye?'

It's the fallout with the kids that's torturing her the most, and her being hurt in this way is breaking my heart for all of them, her kids AND her!"

I empathized, of course, and we talked about how complex and difficult her sister's situation was. We commiserated about what resources there might be for the children besides their mom, and we discussed what support might be available for my friend's sister. It was a long walk.

Several weeks later, my friend and I had lunch. I asked about her sister. She said, "She's coping pretty well, all things considered. She has a good job, thank God, so she's not going to starve, but her two girls, who are nine and six, are really worrying her. I'm here to tell you, Mischa, the nine-year-old, is nine going on 40. She's a pistol, acts totally pissed at her dad all day, but then calls out for him in her sleep. My sis is freaked about what this whole situation is doing to the girls psychologically because they pick up every emotion she's having, and it's a real emotional smorgasbord inside her, as you can imagine. Last night she asked me if I thought she should take them to a therapist or have them talk to the school psychologist."

"What did you tell her?"

"To get all the support possible for all three of them!"

"What about the 6-year-old?"

"Kara's just clinging to my sis. She's afraid to go to school, watching her sister and mom with huge eyes every

minute. But what worries my sis the most is that she's suck-
ing her thumb again, dragging her 'blankie' around everywhere, and she's wet the bed twice, which she hasn't done for
two years!"

"Sounds pretty understandable to me," I said. "Coming
home from my first week ever at camp and finding my dad
gone and thinking maybe he didn't ever want to talk to me
ever again would make *me* want to suck my thumb and hug
my 'blankie'!   I'd probably want to sleep so hard that a full
bladder wouldn't wake me up either!"

My friend laughingly agreed.

A week later, I got a call at my office from my friend's
sister, Lila. "Margie [my friend] told me that you do rituals
for closure with people. I don't know how much she's told
you about what's going on with me, but I think my girls and
I really need to do something like that."

I told her that Margie had kept me pretty well up-to-date
and that I'd be more than happy to talk with her about the
possibilities of a ritual that might help the three of them in
their process of moving forward. We made a date for coffee
to talk about it.

At the coffee shop, I asked her, "Lila, what was it about
the idea of a ritual that appealed to you?"

"When she said that you help people bring destructive
things to an end without 'trashing' anyone, I thought, 'Wow,
do we need that!' I feel so many negative things about Bob

that it's spilling over to the girls, and they're feeling their own negative feelings. He's becoming the boogey-man for all of us. I know that's not productive, but I don't know how to stop the cycle. It's mushrooming by the day."

"Do you know if he plans *ever* to contact the girls?" I asked.

"I can't imagine that he won't—he adores them, but I have no idea when. So for now, I think I have to deal with *what is* with the girls for all of us to stay sane."

I told her, "I understand. In any case, I believe that finding a balance between letting go and revaluing what one chooses to keep from any relationship that has ended fulfills a basic need, both psychologically and spiritually. I think that a mistake we all-too-often make, both as children and as adults, is to resort to either/or thinking, dualistic extremes of idol or villain, when our feelings change about another person. What I've found is that making the space and time to say clearly what is true 'in both columns' (what we don't like, what we still like) is very grounding and settling, both for kids and grown-ups. And that's the core of any ritual for closure that I co-create with people."

"I think this would be really helpful for Mischa and Kara right now, and I know it would be good for me to do! I can hardly think of one good thing about Bob at the moment," she responded, laughing. Lila had the same musical laugh as Margie's, and we agreed that "forgetting" is one of the most common results of pain and disappointment. We planned a simple ceremony together, and made plans for sharing it with her children.

The next Friday afternoon, per our agreement, I met Lila at her house and we went together to pick up Mischa and Kara from school. I found the girls delightful, spontaneous and verbal. "Hi! Mama told us we get to pick out our favorite flavor of ice cream and then tell you everything we think about Daddy," Mischa said the minute she bounced into the back seat.

"Yes, that's right! So what's your favorite flavor?" I grinned at this little spontaneous-combustion machine.

"Well, last week it was chocolate chip, but I don't know yet what it is this week," she mused, and just then Kara chimed in, "Mine's chocolate! I'm Kara."

"Hi, Kara! Mmm, I love chocolate too!"

We all got an ice cream cone and enjoyed our treats thoroughly on the way back to their house. Lots of moans of delight and good-spirited arguing about the "best" flavor of all filled the car. When the car stopped, Kara asked, "Do we have to get sad now?"

"Good question, Kara," I replied. "I believe what we're going to do now will probably have both sad feelings and happy feelings in it, and that we'll just be together with them so they're safe to feel. Does that sound OK?"

"Yeah, I can do that, can you do that, Mama?" she said in her six-year-old wisdom and candor, watching her mother's face for clues.

Her mom and I smiled at each other. "Yes, baby," Lila said, "I can do that, too. And I'm glad Monza's here with us so we can all feel safe to feel whatever we're really feeling."

When we got inside, Lila asked the girls, "Where would you like to do our ceremony?"

Mischa and Kara looked at each other, then Mischa went over to Kara and whispered in her ear. After Kara nodded vigorously, Mischa said, "We wanna talk in our bedroom 'cuz it's where we feel all our mixed-up feelings most, when we're going to sleep and just waking up."

We all gathered in their room, each girl on her twin bed and each adult on a chair next to the beds so that we made somewhat of a circle.

I said, "Let's close our eyes and breathe some deep breaths to get relaxed and still inside." After a few breaths, I began, "You can open your eyes now, and I hope you'll stay relaxed as we talk about how you're feeling since your dad left while you were gone to camp. When you came home and found out that your mom and dad are getting a divorce, all three of you have been having lots of feelings.

What we want to do is to give you a chance to say some important things to each other about how you're feeling, and I also hope you'll give each other some ideas about how you'd like it to be for the three of you together from today on. Maybe there are some things you've been doing or saying that you want to stop; maybe there are some things you haven't been doing or saying that you want to begin. We're just going to take some time to be honest with each other, to say what you're mad about, sad about, and glad about. And I think doing that always makes us feel better, even if it's hard to do sometimes."

"So, Lila, since you're the mom, let's start with you. Are there some things you'd like to say to the girls about what you've been feeling or are feeling?"

"Yes," she replied, "I've been feeling angry about your dad, and I know I've been saying some pretty mean things in front of you girls. I'm sorry that I've blurted out disrespectful words, like 'bastard' and 'ass,' and even though I don't think it's wrong to feel angry, I promise you both that I will try my best not to say disrespectful things about your dad anymore when you have to hear me. I know he's your dad, and you deserve to have me show respect for him. I still believe he's very happy we had each one of you, and I *know* we were very, very happy when we created you and when you were born. I think he has a lot of good traits that you should know I recognize." Lila paused, and it seemed she was struggling—then she looked directly at me with a little panic, as if saying, "What now?"

I asked her, "Lila, what are some of the good traits about Bob that you want Mischa and Kara to know you value in him?"

Looking relieved and grateful for the prompt, Lila went

on. "I think your father is basically a very intelligent man, a hard-working man who is really committed to his job and likes what he does. He's an expert sailor and swimmer— that's probably how you became a water-baby, Mischa—and you know how he loves the water, and he is a talented artist—Kara, I think your love of drawing cartoons comes from your dad. He's a good man in lots of ways, and I want you girls to remember that I'm glad he is your dad, even if I'm disappointed and angry about some of the things he's done recently. OK? I think that's enough for me to say right now."

I turned to the girls. "OK, Mischa and Kara, do you have any questions of your mom right now, or are there things you'd like to say about what you like about your dad?"

Mischa blurted, "Yeah, Mama, do you want us to try to forget how much Daddy's hurt you and us so we won't hate him?"

Lila answered carefully, "Good question, baby. No, I believe the work each one of us needs to do, and that's part of why we're having this ritual with Monza today, is to remember the hard things *and* the good things all at the same time. They're *all* true. They're hard to hold in our minds and hearts together sometimes, at least they are for me, but it's the only way to keep it true, to be honest with ourselves and each other. It's funny. You're more worried about how he's hurt me, and I'm more worried about how he's hurt you girls."

Kara said, "I don't know if I have a big enough brain to hold all my love-thoughts and my hate-thoughts!"

Both Lila and I laughed at this child's brilliant candor. I said, "We're laughing because we know just what you mean! We sometimes wonder the very same thing! And you said it perfectly! Do you want to say out loud some of your love-thoughts and hate-thoughts?"

The girls looked at each other, then at their mother. "Mama," Mischa asked, "is it OK if we say some bad words? We've been telling each other how we feel, but we use some bad words when we're alone. If we promise we won't use these bad words except with each other or in this honesty ritual, can we say how we really feel?"

Lila replied, "I think that under these special circumstances that will be all right."

"Well," Kara said, "I'm so mad at Daddy right now I hate his guts. He's a poop-head to be so chicken that he couldn't even say goodbye to us to our faces. I can't even believe a grown-up can be such a chicken! He's more of a chicken than me, and I'm only six! And I wish he was dead instead of just somewhere else because then I wouldn't have to wonder why he stopped loving you and stopped loving us. He'd just be dead but still loving us. I hate him and I still love him, and that's what I hate most of all. I wish I just felt one way or the other!"

Mischa took a deep breath and said, "Me too! I can still smell his aftershave in his closet even with his clothes gone, and I can hardly stand it. He's here at the same time he's so gone. It hurts so much that I want to stick pins in him and put a curse on him so he'll never have anybody love him like we did. He deserves it 'cause he made us hurt and you hurt, Mama. I hate his guts so much I'd like to throw his old innards to the sharks."

Lila kept her gaze steady and nodded as her daughters spoke their truths, even though some of their images threatened to make her (and me) smile. I said, "I believe that feelings, even very painful ones, are not dangerous unless we try to stuff them inside, keep them secret, or pretend they're not real. You have been brave to tell your mom and me the truth about what you're feeling. And now you have two grown-ups who can hold the truth with you. And another thing about feelings: they shift and change. You feel this way today, but it will be OK if the feelings change in time. Whatever you feel is your property, it's your right to experience and express. And your mom and I believe that telling our feelings is one of the most important ways we begin to heal our hurt. I'd like to suggest that all three of you might feel closer by sharing these feelings, by admitting out loud that you're hurting and that you want to feel better, and that you'll work together to remember the good things about your dad even while you're feeling sad and mad about what he's done recently."

I had noticed something that had come up that I felt quite certain Lila would agree with my adding in, but I wanted to check it out with her before I went on. So I said, "Is it OK with you girls if I ask your mom a private question?"

"Sure," they replied.

Whispering in Lila's ear, I asked, "Is it OK if I pick up the issue of cowardice and deal with it here right now?"

"Absolutely," she nodded, "go wherever you think might help."

I said, "I just wanted to check something out with your mom that we hadn't talked about before. Since she says it's OK, I'm going to ask the three of you to make one other promise: Will you, Lila, Mischa, and Kara, all promise that even when you feel scared about anything that's happening, you'll try your best to be courageous instead of cowardly and bring it up to talk about honestly among the three of you? Knowing that you've been hurt by your dad's being 'a chicken,' as you put it, will you try your best not to be cowardly with each other?"

"Yes, we promise," they all said solemnly.

"And even though I'm asking that," I went on, "I'd also like it if you'd try to notice times when you do feel afraid to say what you really feel, or maybe to stand up for someone who's being picked on at school. If you do both—be courageous when you can and notice when you can't—I think that helps to learn not to be too afraid to do what you believe is right. And you can also understand better how all of us sometimes get too afraid to be brave in the ways we'd like.

I got up from my chair, went around the circle, and put my hand gently on Lila's head, on Mischa's head, and then on Kara's head. "Now I pray that each one of you will be blessed with feelings of love, security and peace, knowing that you have each other, that you can tell each other the truth, and that you don't have to feel alone while you go through this big change in your lives. May it be so."

I added, "If you want to feel these feelings, I invite you to say, 'May it be so.'"

"May it be so," the three of them replied. Then this brave mother and her brave daughters hugged each other tightly.

Guidelines for an Informal Ritual with Young Children

1. Whenever possible, make sure children help to direct how the ritual is carried out. You might ask:

   a. where would you like to do the ritual?

   b. what time of day do you feel would be best for you?, and

   c. what, if any, special things would you like to bring, or be sure to do?

   Once you have asked them, be sure to remember and do what they request.

2. Even when structuring a ritual for a parent and children, the ritual may be focused primarily on facilitating the children's ability to state all their feelings.

   a. It is important to give children permission to express their feelings uncensored.

   b. In many cases, the children may not need to process the feelings, at least not until some other time, and, even then, only in bits and pieces.

      i. Just learning to accept and express the reality of having strong, yet contradictory feelings can be deeply healing.

      ii. Learning that both adults and children can sometimes be brave and sometimes not is another important piece of wisdom to acquire.

3. You can spontaneously add additional pieces to the ritual if any of the children express a feeling or need that can be addressed by ritual.

CHAPTER 8

Divorce In Which One Parent Completely Abandons the Children: Ritual for Young Children

Joel   Gideon, 5   Sarah, 3

local rabbi, a friend, called me with a problem he said he'd never come up against before. A member of his congregation had a son who was no longer observant, who'd married, and now was alone with two children because his wife had left without warning, saying she "just didn't want to be married or a mother any more." He said, "This woman in my congregation, those kids' grandmother, is bereft; she doesn't know what to do for her son or her grandchildren, and, of course, she considers it a spiritual crisis I should have the answer to."

"I understand your predicament," I said. "I think we'd both agree it *is* a spiritual crisis for all of them, but I also think our solutions might have nothing whatsoever to do with the solutions this dad and his kids need to find for right now." I continued, "If you feel close to this young man, even if he no longer participates in the life of your synagogue community, I think it would be a loving gesture to call him, give him your support, tell him simply that you're thinking of him in this challenging time and that you'll be giving his mother all the support you can while he makes his way."

"That's exactly what I'll do!" he said. "I taught that kid Hebrew every Friday afternoon for six years. I think I sometimes feel so cautious that people will think I'm trying to get them to 'come back to the fold' that I forget I can just say 'I care.'"

"It's an occupational hazard," I said. "I remember my own dad struggling with how much to initiate contact with people who'd left the church. He didn't want to harass them, or make them feel he disrespected their choices. But he didn't want them to think he didn't care, either. It's a tough call."

Several weeks later I got a call from a man named Joel. When he said, "My former rabbi, Levi Spelman, suggested I call," I knew right then this was the young man my friend and I had been talking about.

It turns out Joel had called the rabbi back after he received his initial "I care" call. He trusted the rabbi's integrity enough that he did not feel pressured to come back to services; he was wise enough to realize he was being given a resource he hadn't considered was still available to him. Rabbi Spelman had told Joel that I was an inter-faith resource for people going through divorces, and that I might have some ideas for how to get through this with his children so that their suffering was alleviated in some ways.

"My kids are a mess. They're only five and three. I have a great nanny, but they're both wetting the bed every night, crying over every little thing, and showing huge anxiety over where I am at every moment. Of course they can't understand at all where Mommy is, and they ask 50 times a day 'When's Mommy coming back? Where's Mommy, Daddy? When's Mommy coming home?' It's killing me."

"I'm so sorry, Joel. I can only begin to imagine how brutal this feels to you." I took several deep breaths. "I'm sure this process will take a lot of time, and that you'll probably need help from several resources. For one thing, I want you to have the name of an amazing play therapist I know here in town who does profoundly healing things with little children who've experienced trauma. I think she'd be very helpful to you and your little ones. And I also know a fellow whose therapy practice is specifically with men who are raising children on their own. He might have helpful ideas for you, too, as well as particular understandings and resources I don't know about. I'll give you those names if you want them."

"I'll take all the help I can get. I'm drownin' here." He really sounded exhausted and panicked.

"What are your children's names?" I asked.

"Gideon is the older, Sarah is the younger."

"Thanks," I said, "I like to refer to them by name. What

I can offer you, Joel, are some ideas of things you can do with Gideon and Sarah right now, even though they're little, that may help them feel more grounded, more secure, more sure of *something* even when there's a lot that's uncertain for them. Because they *are* so young right now, my instinct says that you'll probably have to do, over the years they're growing up, several versions of what I do, but it's never too early to start. Would you like to talk about it now, or would you like to come to my office for a more extended conversation?"

He said, "I'd like to talk to you face to face. And I've got to get to work anyway right now. How about I take off work a little early on Friday and we talk?"

When we met on Friday afternoon, I could tell immediately that Joel was an earnest, if utterly overwhelmed, young man. He arrived exactly on time, but seemed nervous and looked a little disheveled. I tried to put him at ease right away by giving him a cup of coffee and some cookies, all the while asking him about his work. I found out he was only 32 and owned his own software design firm. He relaxed pretty quickly.

When we shifted to the issue of his children, I said, "What I try to do is find ways to honor the emotional, ethical, and/or spiritual realities of the crisis of a break-up in ways that are healing both for parents and for kids. And I don't believe they have to be addressed in any prescribed language (such as Jewish, Christian, Buddhist, etc.). Since your children are so small, I think the key here is 'keep it simple.'"

"Simple is about all I can do right now anyway, so that's good," Joel smiled as he took a sip of his coffee.

I went on, "The goal, the one and only goal, is to tell your children what is true in a way they can grasp at their ages. For example, would you tell me what you think would be the most important things you could say to them right now?"

"Well," Joel paused and looked out the window, "that I love them with all my heart ... that they're safe with me ... and safe with Erica, their nanny ... they don't need to feel afraid of lots more changes. I want them to know that we are going to keep doing the things we always do, like make blue-berry pancakes on Saturday mornings, play in the park and swim on Sundays, have tuna casserole on Tuesdays, have story time every single night, that stuff, as well as make lots of space for them to talk about what they're feeling since Mommy has gone away." Tears came to his eyes.

I'm very moved by what you just said. It's simple, yet profound—just what they need. I do have a few other ideas I'd like to share with you, if you'd like. But for now, go on, if you will."

"I also want them to know that Nana and Papa are still going to play with them just like always. We'll keep going to their house and they'll come to ours, and that Gideon and Sarah will keep going to their friends for play dates. Just say how many things are *not* changing.... But what can I say that's true about their mom? I don't even know where she is, for godsakes."

"What do you know, Joel?" I asked.

He replied, "She just left a message on my phone at work: 'I don't want to be married to you or to be a mom anymore. You've always been better at it anyway. Don't try to get me back, Joel. I just need to be free. Please get a divorce and find somebody you'll be happy with.' I've got it memorized, as you can see."

"Whew," I stared into space, "that's pretty final."

"Yeah, you could say that." He huffed and shook his head.

"Regarding what to say to the kids right now, Joel, I think the fact that she's gone is the crucial matter. The why's and wherefore's are too complex for children that young, I think. There will be plenty of time for that. Right now, they need to know that the parent they have is a parent 'for keeps.' Lots of kids have one parent; they probably even have some friends with single parents. I might consider mentioning that. Other than what you're saying about 'she's gone away,' I believe that if you do work with the play therapist I mentioned, you and she might explore other things to tell them as issues come up that need attention. I believe that you need to let kids lead at their ages. They'll ask what they're ready to know—that's my experience."

"So, what are your ideas?" he asked.

I suggested that he incorporate a couple of focused rituals within their nightly before-bed rituals of talking and stories: "nightly nuggets" and "what changes/what stays the same." These are helpful rituals for children at any age, I have found, and especially for kids undergoing deep changes.

The principle of "nightly nuggets" is that each person in the circle, including the adult, says (1) what he/she found hardest in the day and what she/he wants to learn from it, and (2) what he/she found best in the day and why it made him/her happy. It's a great way to think back over a day in a balanced way, discerning how everyone finds good and bad in every day, normalizing the flow of positive and negative in everyone's day, be they adult or child. In the situation Joel's family is in, it gives focus for all of them to share their challenges and their triumphs.

The ritual of "what changes/what stays the same" is another way to balance seemingly paradoxical realities. For Gideon and Sarah, their mother leaving certainly can make them fear that everything is changing since some anchor so great has been yanked up in their young lives. That is, of course, true, and needs to be acknowledged. But, as I told Joel, the one "red flag" I saw when he shared with me what he wanted to tell them was that his total focus on "things staying the same" could make his children afraid of change, some of which is a good thing— even in times of turmoil. So I asked him to think of positive changes that he and his children were making that he might intersperse with the affirmations of not-changing.

"I see what you're saying," Joel reflected. "I hadn't thought of that at all."

I said, "I think it would be unlikely that you *would* have thought of it. You're traumatized and wanting your kids to feel safe. I think that's part of why I believe it really does take a village—not only to raise a child—but to help us all get through crises in ways that are empowering instead of destructive."

Since we agreed that Joel would take it from there, I wasn't surprised when I didn't hear from him again. Several weeks went by. Then I had a call.

"Monza, this is Joel. I wanted to give you an update."

"I'm so glad! I've been thinking of you three! How's it going?"

"Gideon and Sarah *love* 'nightly nuggets' and 'what changes/what stays the same'! I think they especially like that I share too; Gideon said the other night, 'Daddy, I like to know about your day!' And every night they come up with new things that they like that are changing. That has really amazed me! They've both stopped wetting their beds almost entirely, for one thing. Sarah has a couple more times, but Gideon doesn't at all if he pees just before bed.

"And when I shared, 'I'm changing into a cook, and I'm liking it more and more,' Gideon said, 'Mommy would sure be surprised,' and both kids giggled. We all laughed. I held my breath, thinking they might start thinking about her being gone and get upset, but they just went right on. It's the first time I've heard them refer to her in a normal way. It was pretty incredible.

"I also wanted you to know that they've insisted that when they stay overnight with my folks they make Nana and Papa do 'nightly nuggets' and 'what changes/what stays the same.' And my parents, believe it or not, are getting 'into it.' The other day my dad actually said, 'Joel, this 'nightly nuggets' idea is very wise, I think.' Amazing—he's not one to give compliments."

"This is really, really good news, Joel. I'm so happy for you and for Gideon and Sarah."

"Oh, and one more thing," Joel said. "We've started therapy, all three of us. The kids with the play therapist, and I'm talking to the guy you recommended who works with single dads. And we talk about what we're learning some nights, too. Gideon said the other night, 'Daddy, I think us going to therapy is both something changing *and* something staying the same.' I asked, 'How so?' and his answer amazed me. He said, 'Cause we're all getting happier, so that's a change, and we're working together as a family, and that's the same. Right, Daddy?' I just hugged him for a long time, nodding. I couldn't really speak."

"Yeah, I'm always amazed at how astonishingly brilliant kids are. They move me to tears when they just pop out with bits of wisdom that take us, as adults, so long to learn, or remember."

"That's it. It's like they're enlightened."

"Absolutely. Joel, I'm really happy that you called."

One day a few months later I saw Joel and his kids in the grocery store. They were in a "serious confab" over what kind of cereal to buy.

"Oh, hi, Monza!" Joel exclaimed when I touched him on the shoulder. "Glad to see you! This is Gideon, and this is Sarah." The kids looked up from the cereal boxes and smiled.

"How are things?" I asked.

"Plugging along," he replied. "Gideon and Sarah are 'playing' every Wednesday with Mrs. Callahan [the play therapist] and like her a lot!"

"Yeah," Gideon chimed in, "Mrs. Callahan has tons of cool action figures to play with. I like those the best." He grimaced, taunting Sarah a little bit, "Sarah likes the *dollies*."

Sarah ignored him, more interested in asking me, "Do you know Mrs. Callahan?" She looked a little puzzled about how I could possibly know *their* friend.

"Yes, Sarah," I replied, "Mrs. Callahan is a friend of mine, too. But I've never gotten to play with her stuff in her office. You're lucky!"

"Yep." She went back to the cereal boxes.

"Well, see you, Joel. Keep up the good work." I moved on down the aisle.

I do not pretend to know all of the complexities of the

changes Joel, Gideon and Sarah had undergone or still may need to undergo. But I do know that when I saw them in the store that afternoon, Joel seemed relaxed, he and his children were carrying on, being a family, and the children were able to be concerned about kids' things: what brand of cereal to buy, going grocery shopping with their dad, and having fun every week with an adult who had great toys to play with.

Guidelines for a Ritual and/or Conversation with Small Children Who Have Been Abandoned by a Parent

1. Have a focused conversation with the child(ren) about what will stay the same, given that security is paramount in the midst of recovering from trauma.

   a. Do this in a warm, but matter-of-fact way; if you try too hard to reassure, or if you convey worry, it will have the opposite effect.

   b. Invite the children to add to your current list of what is remaining the same as they notice. This helps them focus on sources of security, rather than fear.

2. Be honest about the parent being gone, but don't try to explain it too specifically. The child(ren) will ask for what they need as time goes on.

3. Incorporate some ritual, game, or conversation that balances looking at the things that change as well as those that stay the same, so they see change as positive and don't start to fear all change.

4. "Nightly Nuggets" is a ritual that not only keeps children and adults focusing their attention on the present, but it

also brings the adult's life into reciprocity with the children's, a powerful learning model for both.

CHAPTER 9

Divorcing Parent and Step-Parent Send Letter with Key Qualities of a Ritual to College-Age Children

Carmen and Beth   John, 21   Anita, 19

One Saturday, on a winter afternoon, I had a surprising call from a former student. In the course of that call Carmen, a mature woman, reminded me she had fulfilled her English requirement with my courses on her way to a degree in accounting. The fact that a former student called was not the surprise. What *was* surprising was that she asked if I'd be willing to talk with her and her partner, Beth, about how to "break up in a way that was compatible with their beliefs." Carmen said, "I've never forgotten a comment you made one day in class about integrity, in which you said that very thing. You said probably the best test of how well we hold to our values was if a person could 'break up [with a partner] in a way compatible with her beliefs.'" I didn't remember saying it, and I thought (as I had a thousand so many times) how fascinating it is what a student remembers from all the words we professors say.

She went on, "I also remember that you're a minister, so I want to know if you'd be willing to counsel us. We know we need to 'get a divorce' but we don't know how to do it *well*. Could you help us?"

"I'd be honored to try," I replied.

The couple came to my house for our meeting. Carmen, an accountant with a large firm now, was dressed in a stylish business pantsuit and low heels; Beth was dressed in jeans, flannel shirt, and tennis shoes. They had both just come from work. When I asked what Beth's line of work was, she replied, "Assembly line. 38 years. Santiam Vegetable and Fruit Packing Plant."

In answer to my initial questions, I found out they'd known each other for 21 years. Beth had been married to a man before her relationship with Carmen, and had three children from that marriage: two sons and a daughter, all grown now. Beth and Carmen had met at church in a Bible Study group. They'd been friends for several years when Beth was still married, and Beth had been divorced for two years before she and Carmen got together as partners. Since Beth's oldest son, Carl, had left home at 16 when his parents got a divorce, he had not been a big factor in their 15 years as a couple. Beth and Carmen agreed that they'd raised the other two kids, Johnny and Anita, together. Johnny had been six,

Anita, four, when they became partners. Now 21 and 19, the two younger children were now out of the house.

"What drew you together?" I asked.

Carmen looked at Beth. I sensed she wanted Beth to take all the space she wished to talk because she didn't want the fact that we already knew each other to cause Beth any discomfort, for her to feel "left out" in any way by not having known me previously. Moreover, I had already noticed Beth was less verbal than Carmen, a fact Carmen seemed aware of and sensitive to.

Beth said, "Well, we have our religion in common. We go to Faith Center [a large evangelical church in the city]. When we got to know each other, we had our Bible Study group, a women's softball team we both played on, and we found out pretty early on that we both liked to hike and bike and camp and cook and go to movies. And then we fell in love."

"Did you fall in love before or after you were divorced, Beth?"

"Good question." Beth frowned. "When I look back on it now, I'm sure the answer is 'before,' but I didn't let myself admit it until I was divorced. Carmen had become my best friend, that's how I saw it. And she never suggested anything more, did anything, until a year and a half after my divorce was final. She'd had another long relationship with a woman before me, so she knew what was really happening, I think." She looked at Carmen and grinned.

"How was it for you, Carmen?" I turned to bring her into the story-telling.

"Well, I feel exactly like Beth about how we were first drawn together. The other part for me is that I loved her kids. I loved being part of a family. Still do, for that matter. I think I wanted to be partners so that we could both be parents for her kids, for Johnny and Anita. And we had the same ideas, I thought, about child-rearing, money, the importance of giving kids a good start in life, teaching them how to be good people. I guess the one other thing I'd add is that, from the get-go, we liked the same TV shows, the same magazines, and we're both pretty passionate about our politics, hold the same views on that score."

"OK, thanks," I said, "that helps me get a picture of the beginning. Now how would describe what stayed good for you during those 15 years?"

Beth said, "You go first this time, Carm. I want off the 'hot seat.'"

Carmen looked at the ceiling a moment, then said, "Well, like I said, raising the kids together was mostly good. I liked our house being 'Grand Central,' where the neighborhood kids and school pals could hang out, feel comfortable."

Then Beth jumped in, "Yeah, we make a mean pot of Sloppy Joes or spaghetti, and I can barbeque to beat the band." They both chuckled. Then Carmen went on, "Yeah, food and kids, that took a lot of our disposable income and time. I feel pretty good about that, although we had some serious disagreements over money, I don't mind admitting."

"Yeah, well, show me a couple that doesn't bitch about money," Beth muttered. "And for a long time our incomes was pretty different."

I thought I saw a look of irritation pass quickly across Carmen's face. "Then I got my degree to be an accountant, something I'd always wanted to do. You know, Monza, during that time I took classes from you. Beth was supportive of that, mostly; at least she knew I needed to do that for my own self-respect. I'd always been great at math through school, but I spent the first part of my adult years job-hopping, just earning money at jobs below my ability to pay bills when what I really wanted was a career. We had some conflict over how much time I spent on my studies, but for the most part we supported each other pretty well through those years."

I looked at Beth. "And what would you say?"

"Yeah, we did good with the kids. We gave the kids a lot of good times, and we enjoyed ourselves too, I think, at least a lot of the time. And I'm glad Carm got her accounting degree now. At first I gave her crap about gettin' high and mighty, leavin' her roots. But then I figured, if that's what she needs to be happy it's gotta be OK by me. And she did seem a lot happier.

"I didn't like her being gone so much, and I bitched at her sometimes about studying too much, but we was always pretty peaceful, though. We didn't fight in front of the kids—

ever. I think the reason Carl [oldest child] took off so young was that he hated his father for the way he treated me, all the fightin' and bickerin.' When we was getting divorced, Joe and me, I think he figured I'd just get with another angry man, so he split."

"How's your relationship with Carl now?"

"We don't really have a relationship ... and that makes me sad. When he took off at 16, he joined the Marines, and after he got out, he went to Trade School, did his apprenticeship as a plumber, got a job, and got married. In Wyoming. Lives as if he has no mother. I got two grandkids I've never seen. About ten years ago he told me he hates queers. I guess he talked to his little brother or sister on the phone some time when I wasn't home. 'Course he doesn't have anything to do with his dad, either, since they was always oil and water. His kids must think he was hatched from an egg under a stump. Anyways, I pray for him, I hate not knowing my grandkids, but I gotta respect his choices."

"Thank you for sharing this with me, Beth. How hard is it for you to not see your son and grandkids?

"It hurts a lot when I think about it, but I try not to dwell on it." Beth suddenly seemed very, very tired. I got the feeling she had just done more talking in a half-hour than she usually did in a day.

"So, Beth and Carmen, what has happened that brought you to a point where you want to separate?

Beth looked at Carmen, and seemed to pick up her

stream of thought from when she was talking about Carmen's return to school. "Well, you did change. When you was in school, I thought how you seemed different was just 'cause you were studying so hard, and we'd go back to the way we was when you got done with school. But then when you started working as an accountant, it didn't change. You were just more interested in work, didn't want to play baseball much any more, and you wasn't into politics so much. I guess in a way, I did feel like you thought you was better than me now."

Carmen looked tenderly at Beth, a little sad, reflective, as if she recognized something in their relationship *had* been lost because of changes she'd made.

Carmen said only, "I think we did drift apart during that period of school, and then my job demanding so much." She went on, "It feels ironic to both of us, after all these years, especially now that the kids are gone and we've gone through a lot with them. They're finally out of the house, and now we find, just when we have time for ourselves, that we'd both just rather be alone or with other people. We have changed, both of us, wouldn't you say, Beth?"

Beth shrugged, "I guess we prob'ly have."

From my own perspective, I saw the struggle of two people who were now separated by education and profession. There was now a class difference between them, and they'd been unable to keep the kind of closeness they'd had before. I see some people who can survive such changes, and others who can't. I didn't know that for sure; perhaps it was the kids that had held them together so long. But when they grew up and left, Carmen and Beth felt an emptiness that went deeper than the "empty nest syndrome." My best guess is both factors played a role. I made the decision not to take the conversation to a deeper level about what caused them to move emotionally apart from each other.

Carmen continued, "We worked for awhile with a Christian counselor, who wasn't all that affirming of our lesbianism, but she did really respect the length of our commitment and how we'd raised our kids in the Church. We went to her wanting to iron out our difficulties from the basis of our faith, but still we've started to do and say more and more hurtful things. We've been sniping at each other, putting each other down, and leaving without saying 'good-bye' or when we'll be back. We both agree we just can't do it anymore. We're hurting each other, certainly not loving each other, by hanging on like bulldogs, just out of fear of not being Christian enough. And what's Christian about that?"

I could see how much pain they were in, and felt the strong desire they had, even now, to not hurt each other. I asked them, "How do you envision breaking up in a way that is compatible with your beliefs?"

Carmen replied, "It's that matter of that 'integrity' I mentioned to you in my phone call (Bethie was right beside me when I called, by the way). Neither of us wants a divorce, on some level, because we don't believe in it... ."

I sat quietly for a moment, taking in the profundity of what Carmen had just said. I'd seen it many times, in my own life as well as others, but I'd never heard it expressed any more poignantly.

Then Beth jumped in, "even though I've already done it once and am about to do it again. I think of myself as a two-time sinner."

"Well," I said softly, "I hold a different view of that, which I can say more about later, but I want to acknowledge that getting to the point of feeling right about doing something you don't 'believe in' can be excruciatingly difficult. Especially when your heart and mind both tell you that you must do it anyway or lose some part of your integrity. That's a brutal decision." I looked them both square in the eyes, and noticed both of them were tearing up.

Then I suggested, "I think 'divorce' is the wrong word in your case. I think you both are at the place in your lives where you realize you need to 'birth' each other into new life, a next phase of life in which you're not partners anymore. I like that image because, for me, it acknowledges your hard labor, it affirms what you've worked so hard to create and sustain, and it allows you to think of 'letting each other go' in a positive way: in love, with best wishes for happiness and freedom and autonomy, like a mother does birthing a child. What do you think of that idea?"

Beth bowed her head, and her face turned red as if she were about to cry. "That's it. That's exactly what I want it to be."

Carmen added, "Even though I've never actually borne a child, I think it makes so much sense. I don't know why we could never visualize it that way before."

"Well, if it's any comfort," I said, "most of us don't do our most creative thinking when we're in pain, when we're in what my grandma always used to call 'the Deep Muddy.'"

"Beth," Carmen asked, "why does it feel exactly right for you?"

"Well," Beth started tentatively, "because whenever I heard you talk about a ceremony of integrity, I always thought I'd have to say all the stuff I don't like about you or ways you've hurt me and I just don't want to do that. I've already told you. What I *do* want is to send you on your way, and have you send me on my way, with love and strength. You're a good person. I'm a good person. We just don't 'fit' anymore as partners."

The three of us were quiet again, letting that wisdom soak into all of our cells.

I suggested, "So how about your thinking of the kind of birthing ceremony you'd like to create for yourselves? I have a couple of suggestions." Carmen got her pen and paper out, ready to take notes (ever my good student). "I could imagine that, as part of it, you could tell each other, 'Here are the things I want to thank you for over these past 15 years, what I will always be grateful for. Here are my intentions, hopes and dreams for my future for which I would like your blessing, your good wishes." I paused and then added, "you might mark that blessing with some gesture or gift, whatever would make sense to you. How does that sound?"

They both nodded. Beth asked, "Should we do this alone, or should you be our witness?"

"I think you should choose to do it however it feels it most honors you and the sacredness of this decision. I trust you'll decide what's right for you. There is no right way. In my experience, people need different things, but you're getting more and more clarity about what you want, so if you listen to your heart, I believe you'll find the answers there. Take some time to decide about that."

Beth took a big breath. "There's one other thing. And it's big. What can we tell the kids? Johnny and Anita have had us both as moms (they call Carmen 'Mamacita' and me Mama) almost all their lives, and I don't want Carmen to simply vanish when she's one of their moms and always wants to be. I think that's right, isn't it?" Her voice sounded insecure for a moment as she looked over at Carmen.

"Of course, Bethie, I've told you that already ... a hundred times," Carmen replied.

Beth's comment about not wanting Carmen to just "disappear," touched an old wound in me, and I shared with them how passionate I feel about including children, teens, and young adults in the discussion about divorce.

"Where are John and Anita?" I asked.

Beth replied with clear pride, "Anita, my baby, she's in

community college up at Chemeketa, majoring in computer science, and John's in the army.

"Well, instead of trying to call each of them, what about a letter to John and Anita? Perhaps part of your ritual might be to write them a letter together, telling them what you most want them to know. It might be, for the two of you, a way to affirm the connection you *both* will continue to have with them, and I feel pretty certain, from my own experience, that it will mean a great deal to them to hear the truth, whatever it is, from the two of you."

"Hey, you've had two perfect ideas now, the birthing thing and the letter," Beth said, in a teasing tone, flashing a radiant smile that I hadn't seen before. "You 'been around the park,' I can see that."

She went on, "A letter would definitely be the best bet; we could basically send the same letter to both of them. It would give them time to think about it more. Way better than a phone call. I don't want to put them on the spot or freak 'em out worse. It'll be tough on them, for sure. But it's all in how we say it. And Carm's good with words."

At the end of our time together I said it might be good if we could be in touch in a week, so they could tell me if they needed anything more, or what they had decided to do. Just before they got up from their chairs, Beth asked me, "So what's your view of my being a sinner? You're a minister, aren't you? Don't you believe in sin?"

"Ah," I smiled, "I'm glad you remembered to bring that

back up. In a spiritual sense, I *do* believe in the concept of serious error, when we do real harm to another person, but my view of it is probably different from the one your church teaches. I see it as the state of being separate, out of connection, so we act in ways that hurt others. Then we are out of integrity, and out of connection with what I call the Divine—what you call God. So when I do, say, or think things that put me out of connection with the Divine, then I believe I get separated from the Source from which I get the strength of spirit to forgive, be kind, and show real love. I think that's an error in our direction, we're off course in the ocean of highest good for others and ourselves. What you call sinful. When we get off course, we need to get ourselves back on course.

"The reason I don't see you as a sinner as you move through this transition with Carmen, Beth, is that I believe you are moving toward wholeness for yourself and for Carmen, and I know at my core that such wholeness is of the Divine, what God wants for us. In trying to be in integrity you and Carmen are separating so you can keep your caring and kindness for each other, so you can give each other the freedom to grow in the direction each of you needs. So you see, I don't see you as 'sinning' and separating yourselves from God; you're trying to be closer, more in keeping with Divine nature, and—going back to the word that brought you to me—your own integrity."

"Hmm ..." Beth said, in that teasing tone, flashing that

radiant smile for a second time, "kinda loosey-goosey considering how I've been taught, but I sure like the sound of it!" I was still laughing as they walked out my front door, and so were they, probably as much from relief as from her joke.

When I got the call from Carmen the next week, she and Beth had already done what they dubbed their "Divorce Ritual-Birthing Ceremony." They had decided to call their counselor so they could bring their work with her to a close, to affirm to her their desire to see this as a faith-filled gesture, and to stay somehow within their faith tradition, even though they were stretching its doctrinal teachings. I'm happy to say the counselor was very respectful, though initially "challenged" by their terminology. Carmen told me how Beth had quoted me almost verbatim about how they were trying to stay in integrity, kindness and compassion because they wanted to stay in keeping with God's nature.

They had stated their gratitude for each other and their intentions and visions for themselves. The counselor prayed with them. They gave each other a necklace with a cross that said "Hope Eternal" on its back, and they stated they had decided to keep the rings they had given to each other early in their partnership as a testimony to the validity of the love they had for each other.

Then they had read aloud, in front of their counselor, the letter they had written to the young adult children they had raised together. For them, it was a way to bring the children, so important in their lives, into the ritual. Their ritual ended with their counselor offering a blessing on each of them, the couple, and their children.

Beth and Carmen gave me permission to quote their letter:

> Dear John and Anita,
>
> We are writing with some news that is sad <u>and</u> positive for us, but because it impacts you, we want you to know our process. After 15 years, we have both decided that we need to end our relationship as partners, so we will be living separately from now on, but we will <u>not</u> be ending our relationship as your moms. We both feel we have gained wonderful things from each other, and from raising you together to be the great people you are, and now, in order to keep growing, we need to go our separate ways.
>
> We want you to know both of our homes will be your homes. We want you to have keys to both of them, and we want you to know you are <u>always</u> welcome to come home, to either home. We will always be your Mama and Mamacita. Although we won't do things all together like we always have—at least not most of the time, we hope you will choose to include us both together on special occasions in your lives. We would both want to attend, with pride and joy.
>
> We will both contribute to your education, just as we have always planned. We will both help you get started in your adult lives however we can, and we want you to be able to talk with both of us about whatever

issues come up with which you need help.

We have made a will, and you are both legal heirs of both of us. You will <u>always</u> be our children, even when you're old and gray. And we're even older and grayer. Ha ha.

It is a joy and an honor to be your mothers. Please know that we are splitting up because we still care a lot for each other and want each other's best. We don't hate each other, and you will never have to choose one parent over the other in order to be loyal. All we ever want from you is for you to know we love you and want you to be the best person you can be. If you have any questions or concerns, please feel free to write or call either of us. I, Mamacita, will be at XXX (address) and ZZZ (new phone number). I, Mama, well you know my vital statistics. They'll stay the same.

We love you always and forever,
Mama and Mamacita

Guidelines for When Divorce Is an Ethical Conflict

1. Seek out resources/people you respect who can help you look at the issues from different perspectives, so you can see the ethical choices through different lenses.

2. If you decide that staying in the relationship has become progressively destructive and efforts to work through it are not successful, then, using insights from several different perspectives, craft a process for separation that focuses on respect and integrity.

3. If you can, look at the separation as a gift of love, not a hurtful act.

Guidelines for a "Ritual" Letter to an Adult Child Away from Home

Give careful consideration about what to tell any adult children in a letter, by phone or in person. What would be good for one person might be upsetting for another.

If adult children are away from home, you may want to consider sending a letter first, so you can allow them time to absorb the information and take it in, then call you as soon as they want to talk.

Make sure the letter includes the elements that define what will change, what will stay the same, and what commitments the parents are making to the young people. It may also contain a statement of your feelings of sorrow or sadness.

In a phone call, however, since the adult child's initial reactions may not be apparent to the parents, consider a follow-up phone call during which the young adults can express any feelings of their own.

Parents need to give adult children ample time to catch up with them in their emotional process. It may take awhile.

A joint letter from both parents, or the parent and a step-parent, demonstrates a commitment to an ongoing respect and ability to continue to work together, if need be, to support the young adults.

CHAPTER 10

Divorcing Parents with Serious Religious Differences Must Find Mutually Respectful Agreement

Charles and Sandra   Adam, 10   Mark, 9   Luke, 7   Ruth, 5

I got a call from a Judge Marshall, a Family Court Judge, who I knew, by reputation, was very invested in the well-being of the children of divorcing parents. When he told me why he was calling, I was surprised, to say the least! He said he'd been given my name by a local Evangelical Christian pastor. When he said the referring man's name, I thought, "You just never know."

Pastor Benton and I had been part of a Speakers' Bureau during the period when Oregon was dealing with the "No on 9" and "No on 13" initiatives, Anti-Gay legislation that would have ensured that no gay or lesbian person could ever teach in any state grade school, high school, or university. Although "Pastor B," as he was called by his congregation,

and I were on opposite sides of the issue, we had been paired
to speak on several panels and had developed what I thought
of at the time as a grudging respect for each other. We both
held civility and respectful speech as high values, and we had
carried on a vigorous debate while showing that two people
of faith could hold widely differing opinions. We shared a
healthy sense of humor, and I'd wound up liking the guy,
believing he liked me. Now it seemed clear that he had at
least respected me.

Here was the situation: the Family Court Judge was
dealing with a couple with extremely different belief systems,
who were in total opposition about the values they wanted
their children to develop in life *and* how that impacted what
they needed in their daily structure and activities. The judge
believed that the divorcing parents, Charles and Sandra, both
clearly loved their four children. However, in making his
decision about custody and visitation, he was concerned
about the impact on the children of such completely incom-
patible styles of parenting and the degree of conflict the
parents were in over their different value systems.

The judge knew the wife's pastor, who was also very
active (or a visible presence) in the local community. While
he was at a civic event, Pastor Benton approached him and
said he hoped the judge would do the right thing for this
family. The judge said, "I can't talk about the case, but I do
want to see the parents work it out in a way that is good for
the children." He also said, "I asked the pastor if he knew

anyone neutral whom the wife would be willing to work with who might also be acceptable to the husband? The pastor thought for a minute and then said, 'Yes, I do.' He recommended you. Benton said you were open-minded about spiritual values and that you use a vocabulary that might bridge the gap between a person of strong religious faith and someone who had no religion. I checked you out, and I'd like to know if you'd consider working with the parents if I recommend it to them and they agree." I was still a bit stunned that Pastor Benton would refer me to work with one of his parishioners, but I told the judge I was willing to try.

"Good," he sighed. "I'll see if they'll agree to see you and ask for a release so I can give you some background information. It's a tough one. I think you'll see why."

When Judge Marshall called me back, he said the couple agreed to have at least one meeting with me and had given him permission to share some background information. He said, according to my notes:

Charles (father): a nuclear engineer. Calls himself an 'atheist, anarchist, and iconoclast.' Says only thing he believes in is science; no deities, including Easter Bunny, Santa Claus, tooth fairy, or Loch Ness Monster [fun guy]. Sarcastic, calls ex-wife 'Mrs. Thou-Shalt-Not,' 'Mrs. Holy-Holy.' Calls his kids 'Religo-Robots.' Guy is brilliant, rapid-fire wit. Thinks kids would do better with him because he provides much more mental stimulation: board games, computer-time, Exploratorium, museums, planetarium, strict oversight of homework, projects ... THINKING, he says. Says he met his wife in college, knew she went to church but didn't think it was a big deal to her, didn't find out 'til after they were married how into religion she was. Now he thinks that all his ex really wanted was her MRS. Degree. Says she's 'stuck in Little House on the Prairie and they have zero in common.'

Sandra (mother): homemaker, volunteer at her church's Soup Kitchen and Helping Hand Closet. Defines self as 'Fundamentalist Christian, a true believer.' Thinks kids do better with her mostly because 'he's already killed their innocence, does his best to kill their faith.' Hates that he over-schedules them, never lets them have totally free time to 'just play.' Says she can't remember why she and ex got together; just that they seemed to enjoy each other a lot in college, says he used to have a kind heart—always was a brain, but he used to respect her. Now, anything but. She wants kids to have stability, good moral values (right/wrong, good/evil), sense of family harmony (time for FUN), good sense of humor (not sarcastic, mean). Doesn't think kids should be with him half-time because of his influence on them. OK for parts of weekends, some chunk of summer, and some holidays (NOT Christmas, since 'he doesn't even believe in it').

Overall: Both love kids, have *very* different goals for them. Interesting: rules big in both houses, just different ones. Diff. definitions of fun, what's of most value for kids.

First, I spoke with Sandra and Charles individually. What they told me confirmed the intensity of their feelings about their own value systems being the "right" one, the "only way" that could be good for the children. Sandra said, "I can't even talk about Charles without my blood boiling. I have to confess, sometimes I call him the Anti-Christ. But I know it's not Christian of me … it's just killing me to put our babies through this, and I can't control his mouth. He'll do everything in his power to destroy their faith, and he's killing their spirits too. Each of them has come home from staying with him, devastated by something he said that crushed their belief in … in … " she threw her hands out, shaking her head in total frustration, "anything, *anything* from Santa Claus to God.

"They come back to me asking, 'How come Daddy says only stupid people or scared people believe in God, Mommy? Does Daddy think you're stupid and scared?' I have to confess, I've lashed back, telling them that he's the one who is stupid. Then I try to backtrack and say, I didn't really mean that. But I try to make them keep believing that God is real and that they need to believe that Jesus died to save us from our sins." Sandra was clearly in despair over what might happen to her children's very souls because of her husband's influence.

When I spoke with Charles, he said, "I'm so sick of Sandra's 'sweetness and light' that I can't think straight. Sandra and I live on different planets. Or in different centuries! I get so furious when I think she doesn't want me to ever be with my kids because she thinks I'll ruin 'em, or take them away from her precious Jesus. They'll be working in a soup kitchen for minimum wage when they grow up if she has her way. It's all about God and service to others in her book, no learning computer skills, or science, really no *learning* at all unless it's about her mythical god. How did we ever get married? I must have been insane. Actually, despite her 'Christian Values,' I think we got married because she manipulated me, hid from me her fundy beliefs until she got me to marry her. Wonder what God would think of that?" He laughed, with a charming smile and sarcastic tone.

As I talked with Sandra and Charles, I asked each the same questions:

"What do you think the odds are of [Charles] [Sandra] changing?"

"Do you think one of you or both of you are fighting for control of what happens to the kids?

"Do you think [Charles] [Sandra] is trying to control you?

"Do you think you are trying to control her/him?

"How aware do you think the kids are of the power struggle the two of you are in over what values and experiences the kids need to be exposed to?

"Do you think both of you or just one of you says stuff to the kids that negates the other person's values?

"What kind of impact do you think it's having on the

kids?"

"How important is it to you to have your children be free of the stress of the conflict between the two of you?

"Do you think you could stop saying things about their other parent if you decided to, or would that be unrealistic?

"Do you believe that your children will ultimately choose what they want to believe as they grow up?

"Are you willing to consider creating some agreements with her/him about how to expose your children to the values and experiences that are important to *you*, without trying to control what the other parent does?

As you might guess, both parents answered the questions pretty much as expected: The other person would never change ... we're both fighting for control of what happens to the kids ... she/he *is* trying to control me ... I'm *not* trying to control her/him ... the kids are totally aware of the conflict and understand it to varying degrees, depending on their age ... they are pretty traumatized and confused, although they do know what they like and don't like about what goes on when they are with each of us ... absolutely don't want the kids to suffer ... want them to be as happy and strong as they can be ... could stop saying things to the kids ... yes, the kids would decide what they are ultimately going to believe ... and yes, if I could find a way to do what I want with the children when I have them and not have her/him undermine it, I'd would consider some kind of agreement.

Both hedged around not talking to the kids about the other parent by wanting reassurance the *other* parent would stop *too*. Both reiterated that they believed strongly that the kids needed to have certain values instilled and certain experiences at a young age. Significantly, however, both seemed more moved to positive action on behalf of their children after they answered the questions I asked.

So often when people are divorcing, their pain is so great that they drag the kids into the middle of things, all the while thinking they are fighting for what is *best* for their kids, to varying degrees, unconscious of the fact that their own war is doing more damage to the children than anything else could. If they have a chance to think about key questions, they can often make shifts that are surprising to anyone who has witnessed the battles.

I asked the parents if I could meet with the children, and they agreed. I found all four children, ages five to ten, to be intelligent, stressed, and pretty clear about how they felt. A few of their comments stand out in my mind.

At one point, Adam (10), said, "I don't really think that either Mom or Dad is totally right about everything. Dad's all big into, 'the world of science.'" He waved his fingers in the air to show quotes. "And with Mom, it's all about God and Jesus and living the Christian life. Ya know?"

Mark (9) chimed in, "Dad acts like a regular old math assignment is the Ten Commandments. We have to memorize multiplication tables during dinner. And Ruthie's only five. Plus, every homework paper he checks like it's going to the Principal. It's pretty intense." I noticed that Mark chewed his nails to the quick, was the slowest to engage in our conversation.

I looked over at Luke (7) and Ruth (5). "Do either of you have anything to add about how you feel about being with your dad and with your mom?"

Ruth said loudly, "I love my mommy and my daddy. The only thing I don't like about going back and forth is I can't always remember what all the different rules are."

Luke said, "One thing I like at Dad's is we don't have to be so churchy. I don't like reading the Bible every day and having family prayer time and memorizing a Bible verse every time we break a rule or get into a fight with each other."

"Monza, do you think Dad or Mom is right?" Mark asked.

I said what I truly believe: "I believe they each have a right to believe what they want, and to share that with you, but they need to respect each other's beliefs in front of you kids. You have the right to decide what you believe when you grow up, but I think it's too confusing to hear totally opposite things from your parents all the time while you're growing up. It's upsetting, I think, to feel caught between them because you love them both, and you want to believe both of them."

"Are you here," Mark continued, "to make my mom and dad get along? If you are … well, good luck!" The other kids snickered.

"Good question, Mark. My answer is 'no.' My job is to see if there might be ways they could set up some guidelines to make things easier for you kids since you have two places that are your homes now. And two parents you love, who love you all very much, but who think very differently about lots of things. You're helping me by telling me how you feel about how it's been so far to live with their conflict."

Luke said softly, "I just wish they didn't hate each other." His brothers and sister all nodded.

"Luke's right, I know. It's so hard to have the two people you've loved all your life hate each other. I can see you're all really good kids, and I know it's sad, this split in your family. If it helps at all to know you're not alone, I think most of us whose parents get a divorce feel that way. I know I felt the same way when my parents got divorced. "

Ruthie suddenly looked up, "Are you OK now? You look like a happy person."

I smiled, "Yes, Ruthie, I am."

She squinted at me, "So it didn't wreck ya, did it!?" We all laughed.

"No, it didn't," I agreed. "But I think it could have been easier. That's one of the reasons I work like this with families. I want to make it as painless as possible for kids. I've really enjoyed meeting you all." They politely came over and shook my hand. All except Ruth, who lunged at me for a big hug.

I left, thinking how challenging this particular rift was. The impact on children of parents having totally different goals for their children was enormous: Charles and Sandra wanted very different things for their children, wanted to spend their money differently on them, use time differently with them, talk differently with them, and teach them totally different beliefs and values. And both of them were cemented in dualistic either/or thinking. One had to be right, the other wrong.

Next, I met with Charles and Sandra together. I shared with them that their answers to the questions I'd asked each of them were pretty much the same. They didn't seem too surprised that each of them thought the other was the most controlling! I shared bits and pieces the children had given me permission to pass on, and I think both parents were sobered and moved by hearing some of their children's struggles and insights.

As we continued, I said, "I believe there is a special pressure on kids when two parents hold diametrically opposed beliefs because they're still forming the ways they see the world and their place in it, how they interpret their experiences. And kids pick that up *first* from their parents. Although it's intellectually fine for a child to be presented with differing viewpoints, it is more complex when kids' parents are hammering them with completely different philosophies, moment by moment, every time they're with one parent or the other. Especially when mocking words of disrespect or disapproval are used regarding the other parent's beliefs.   Then kids are torn: What is RIGHT to believe? Dad's way? Mom's way? They can't choose! And they're ripped up by their loyalty to both parents and their love.   Or, if they do accept one set of beliefs over the other, they often experience it as choosing one parent over the other, so the problem is compounded with issues of loyalty and alienation.   It's only eight more years until Adam's out of the house, on to college.   Ruth has 13 more years.   For the duration, I hope you can work together to find a way to make some basic agreements."

I told them about some other parents who had made some basic agreements, which they stated to their children in front of witnesses. "Could you consider writing out the top three or five requirements you each have for how you could each live your own life with your children without exposing them to conflict over your differences?   Out of that, do you think perhaps we can find priorities you *can* agree on and create a set of guidelines?" They began to make notes.   I went on. "Would you be willing to make these lists, and then come back together to see if we can draft a document you can both keep and consistently follow?"

I concluded, "Our hope is that you can create a statement you might say to your children so the kids can have some safety and ease and won't have to be so afraid that one of you will start lashing out at the other. If you like, you can think of it as 'Articles of Respect.'   I believe that's the best you can do for your children. They'll find their way; they're great kids, but they can't flourish in a war zone. I trust that you know, in your hearts, as well as I do, that open and ceaseless conflict will really damage them. What I would hope for you and them, instead, is that each of you is able to share with your children the values you hold dear, and give them experiences that support those values. From there, they have a foundation to make their own choices.

Both Charles and Sandra acknowledged the sanity of such a plan, and seemed more at peace, even sitting in the same room together, as if the fight had gone out of them. I hoped the feeling would last over time.

Our next meeting was successful, and resulted in a document they both said they could live with in good conscience and by which they could abide.

Here is their document, with their Articles of Respect.

Dear Adam, Matthew, Luke, and Ruth:

We want you to be happy, secure, and free to believe what your conscience guides you to trust. Because we believe different things about the World and our place in it, we know that we have made it hard for you to know who and what to trust. We're sorry for that. As your parents, from this day forward, we promise:

1. We will not mock each other's beliefs in your presence.

2. We will not speak disrespectfully of any activity or idea that the other has introduced you to.

3. We will each simply teach you the values that are most important to us and create life experiences for you that we think you can learn and grow from.

4. We will answer any questions you have about our own beliefs as carefully as we can, and if you ask either of us a question about the other parent's beliefs, we will respectfully suggest that you ask that parent to give you his/her answer.

5. Since we disagree so strongly with each other, we'll not try to discuss the other person's beliefs at all, but we'll make sure you have people you can talk to when you have questions or issues you need to sort through that involve both value systems.

6. We will abide by a schedule that makes sure you have a balance of scheduled activities and free time, plus time to attend activities that are important to each of us to share with you

When Sandra and Charles completed this document, they invited some of their respective family members and friends to be present when they read it, together, to their children. It helped their own community members, some of whom had been as polarized as the parents, to support making each of the children's homes a safe haven, where they could alternately learn and gain experience from each parent's values, rules, and activities.

Guidelines for Parents With Opposing Belief Systems

1. Take time to think carefully about the impact that the conflict over value systems has on the children.

2. Have each parent make a list of priorities of what each one needs in order to live peacefully with the children according to her/his own values without being in conflict with the other parent.

3. Create a document that outlines what the parents will do to (a) share their own values with their children, and (b) avoid being in conflict with the other parent's values.

4. Make sure the list addresses the issue of creating time and space for the children to do the activities most important to both parents (as well as the children).

5. Make sure the document does not require that either parent support or accept the other's values.

6. When conflict over values is extreme, avoid putting either parent in the position of discussing the other parent's value system, but make sure the children have people they can talk to when they have question or issues about how to make sense out of their parents' conflicting values and goals.

CHAPTER 11

One Parent in a Divorcing Couple with Serious Power Differential Clarifies Her Values

Arthur and Madeline   Ben, 14   Carolyn, 10

*M*adeline came up to me at the end of a service at the Unitarian church where I'd just spoken about my work with non-traditional rituals for times of transition. "Do you think it would do any good to do a divorce ritual even though I've already been divorced for six years? In fact, I'm already in a new relationship—a *great* one, I'm happy to say. But there are still some things I really need to resolve, clarify, and make some new intentions about. I didn't even realize how many—although my new boyfriend has tried to tell me, god knows."

"I don't ever think it's too late, Madeline," I replied. "There've been times when it's been years after a relationship of mine ended before I really know what I needed to say."

"That's heartening ... can we have tea sometime and talk about it?"

So we did.

As she took a sip of Licorice Spice tea, Madeline began, "I got divorced from Arthur when my son, Ben, was eight and my daughter, Carolyn, was four. So, thankfully, I didn't stay in a horrible situation 'for the sake of the kids.' But in spite of the fact that we had a no-fault divorce and a judge who made a reasonable decree about custody, our power struggle is still going on *ad nauseum*. I don't want to sound like a victim, but I do still feel like Arthur, my ex, holds all the power and I have none because he makes way more money than I do. He's very well established, a corporate lawyer in the biggest firm in town, and I'm a Head Start teacher. Don't get me wrong, I love what I do, but I just don't make the kind of money Arthur does, and I never will. Of course he does give me good child support so we're not living at the poverty level or anything at our house. But he lives in a house with a pool, game room, and all sorts of stuff the kids love. He buys them every new computer game or gadget they ask for, and he takes them on ski trips on weekends in the winter and boating at Tahoe in the summer. I've asked him to be reasonable about gift giving, and he says just because I'm 'downwardly mobile and proud of it,' I don't need to stifle his generosity. Ugh." She took a breath.

"Do you feel envious of his wealth? Or is it something else?"

"No, I don't envy Arthur ... I wouldn't want to *be* him, that's for sure! I just hate it that he showers the kids with so much stuff, and always has. Then they treat *me* like the 'poor ol' mom who never does anything cool.' And, it's not just that. They have become so 'entitled,' it's like they think they deserve to have anything they want, right when they want it, and they end up treating me like a maid. Ben thinks he's god's gift to the world. He can be so rude and demanding, plus 14 with a vengeance." She rolled her eyes. "Caro acts like a princess, like doing a lick of work is beneath her and that it should be my greatest pleasure to do her bidding. They're not bad kids. It's just that they're so spoiled by their dad and then they make my life miserable. Worse than that, they make my boyfriend's life miserable, too. His name is Ken, by the way. He hates how the kids treat me! They don't backtalk him, but they are so withholding, they just treat him with disdain. *And* he has to put up with their arguing with me and putting me down, and he really hates it. But he gets mad at me, not them. He told me, 'nobody's a doormat if they don't take the floor.'" She moaned, "I guess I *do* sound like a victim. Damn."

"Do you ever set limits on how your kids speak to you?"

"Oh, yeah, I'm not actually passive. Funny, huh, I'm a victim, but not passive? Go figure. I do argue with them a lot, and lecture them about how they need to be more concerned about other people, what's happening in the world, giving something back instead of just taking—being selfish, the whole bit.   I blow up when they won't get off the computer or help with dinner or folding and putting away their laundry. I'm sure they see me as a bitch, but, it's weird, I don't feel like I'm attacking them, I just always feel like I'm defending myself, trying to convince them that my expectations are reasonable, my values about life are important.

"I don't argue with them as much when Ken is around 'cause I'm just trying to keep the peace. We don't live together.   Maybe if we did, he wouldn't think I'm the only one who'll get walked on.

"I guess I do feel too aggressive sometimes—even though at the time it always seems like I'm just defending myself—'cause after I blow up, I always trash myself for not handling it better, and not trusting that they'll absorb my values too, and grow out of being snotty kids.   They weren't *always* this way!"

"When you work with the kids at Head Start, do you assume that they'll just absorb the values you'd like them to have?"

"Um, well, they're littler!   We have to be consistent so they'll know the rules at school ... hmm, I guess I'm not very consistent, am I?"

"What I'm wondering, Madeline, is if you feel that you have the right *and* responsibility to live in your own house by your own values. I'm getting the impression that you have strong values that you believe in, that you're not jealous of what Arthur has, but that you are putting yourself in a one-down position, getting insecure, instead of just taking control of what you want in your own home. Even though you argue with the kids, it's like you need their permission, or at least for them to accept that your expectations are legitimate before you follow through consistently.

"Oh, wow. That's just it, isn't it? Now I see why I've been so confused, feeling like a victim, feeling insecure, and yet upset with myself for being angry and demanding too. It's just been all sort of mixed up. I shift from being angry at myself to mad at them, to defending them to Ken. In all of it, I don't really make the kids do most of the stuff they don't want to do. And I do let them talk to me in ways that are incredibly disrespectful. I think I'm trying to talk them into respecting me and doing things around the house, but why should they if I keep letting things go on that way?

"I don't have to prove anything, do I? Just be who I am and expect what I'd expect of anyone else. You know, I'm not the same person with my kids as I am everywhere else. I'm firm, I'm respected." She smiled slightly. "Actually, people even think I'm fun." She paused, sort of staring off into space, as if trying to take her own insights in more deeply.

After a little while, I asked, "Do you think you can do what you need to in order to make it different?"

She laughed, "Now you're channeling Ken! Seriously, yes, I think a lot of things have just clicked into place. I'm sure I'll still need more help, but I see my way more clearly."

"I'm sure," I said, "that having less access to money than

an ex is hard because it can make you feel insecure, 'cause the kids love the other parent's presents more. Even if you have different values, it's hard not to feel inadequate, assuming the kids will always think you can't measure up. I see it in a lot of divorced families, and I find it painful. What I often see is the parent with less money, or less power in other ways, allows her or his own values and personal power to be undermined. In your case, what kind of a message have you been sending your children about the importance of *your* values and *your* unique gifts, the things *you* are contributing to who they are becoming if you let them exhibit class privilege in your home and keep allowing them to assume that having an 'owning class' dad entitles them to treat anyone with less money, especially their mom, like a slave?"

"Whew. How could I have gone on for years without seeing this clearly?"

"I think it brings that old saying about not being 'able to see the forest for the trees' to mind. When we're in the middle of our own life, it can be incredibly hard to see the patterns. I think you've had a breakthrough today, in seeing your own patterns. You're no longer just seeing it as the kids being rude and privileged because of your ex. You're seeing your own part in it. May I ask you one more question?"

"Sure," she said.

"Do you still feel like a victim?"

"Amazing. No, I don't. Even though I'm stunned that I didn't see it all before, I don't think I even feel angry at myself. Just determined."

It was time for both of us to go, so we left our conversation there. As we walked together toward our cars, I said, "You could just change your behavior, but I think it will be more powerful if you do make it into some kind of ritual. "It can be as simple as saying to your kids what you've recognized, your intention to make a change and why, and then carrying through with your conviction. Something that simple, I've found, can be more transforming than changing piecemeal—and I think you'll encounter less resistance in the long run."

Two weeks later, a xeroxed letter from Madeline arrived in the mail. A post-it note on the top read: "Here's the letter I wrote and read to Ken. Having done that, I feel ready to talk to the kids. I'll tell you how that goes. Thanks with all my heart. Maddy."

Madeline gave me permission to quote her:

On this day, September 4, 20—, I am taking responsibility for my life. I am not a victim of my ex-husband, Arthur, in any way. He can live his life by his values, and I will live, from this day forward, by mine. My life and my children's life in my home will reflect my values: I love simple pleasures and being part of a family who pitches in to get things done and have fun together. I care about sharing love and pleasure more than I do about having things. I want my children to know the worth of my values, as well as my own worth, and I take responsibility that it's up to me to teach them. I promise that I'll make my best effort to set limits that require them to treat me with respect. I will talk to my children respectfully, and I'll expect the same of them. I'll trust in my capacity to be firm, and not get defensive and harsh. I want to take myself lightly, and trust my kids' character, but I hereby take accountability for the development of their character: they aren't finished yet! I still have time to teach them that reciprocity is a higher value to me than entitlement, and that I think they really need to consider their behavior in light of the kind of people they want to be. Ken, I promise that I won't always 'defend the kids' whenever you point out problems you notice; I trust that you have my best interests at heart, and I know that you are much more able to see how I devalue myself by my habitual responses to them. I want to be as happy with my kids as I want them to be happy. I believe that I deserve that. And I know that working toward that goal with my children will make me a better partner to you. I will work every day to fulfill the promises that I make today.

I saw Madeline at church a few weeks later. "Gorgeous letter, Madeline!" I said as I got close to her. "I was deeply touched by it. Thanks so much for giving me a copy."

"Just writing that down and reading it aloud to Ken was *exactly* the *first* 'ritual' I needed. I felt more strength, knowing I had his support to follow through with the kids. A couple days later I was able to read a new version of it to my kids, with the focus on my relationship with them. We had an amazing conversation, and things are actually starting to be different. I never dreamed I'd be able to change the 'set-up.' I just accepted that it was all Arthur's fault and I just had to live with it. I'm so blown away." We hugged each other.

So many times, when I seen people make an internal shift in their minds and hearts, what they seek to change is more successful than they could have imagined. I truly believe that others feel the invisible shift in the person's attitude and it can instantly change the power dynamics. This is not to say that there will be no more struggles, but the essential shift can be permanent.

As I walked away, I reflected—as I have many times before—it actually is, sometimes, just that simple. Not easy, but simple.

Guidelines for Creating Rituals with Children When One Divorcing Parent Has More Power than the Other

1. Examine whether you are feeling like a victim, and thus blaming another person for creating problems in your relationship with your children that you have no control over.

2. Think about whether you are confident in creating expectations based on your own values—for example, about being treated with respect and/or being reciprocal and appreciative.

   a. If you are not doing so, look for ways that you can take accountability for setting up those expectations and following through on them.

   b. Get support and help from others if you need to build your confidence.

3. Create a ritual where you find a time and place to communicate your desire to be more accountable for what you expect instead of blaming your ex-spouse for the problems. Outline how you will change, what new expectations you'll have and what the consequences will be if the children are disrespectful or don't do their share.

   a. Consider writing these intentions in a letter that you will read to your children in person. Let them know you have some things to say/read and that you want to do it without being interrupted.

   b. You can also set up a Family Meeting in which you state

your new awarenesses and requirements. Afterward, the children may have an opportunity to state what they understand about what you are doing and why. This may be appropriate with mature young people.

4. If the children object to the changes you are committed to making, do not argue. This is the moment of truth for you to keep your confidence and just do what you say you are going to do.

CHAPTER 12

Teens in Blended Family Create Ritual after Parents Separate and Take Their 'Own' Children, with No Visitation Planned

Megan, 17   Dierdre, 15

I'd like to dedicate this last story to our youth, to the next gener-
ations. May they reclaim ritual and know more deeply how to
honor life's transitions, so change can more easily foster transfor-
mation and become a path to wholeness.

*M*y meeting with Megan, a high school senior, came
about because Brynn Tillman, a family friend, took me aside
at a birthday party, and said she needed to talk with me about
one of her students. "I have a delightful student who has a
need, and I think you're the perfect person to meet it for her."

"What is it? I'll be happy to help if I can."

Brynn went on, "She wrote a paper about 'family problems' that was absolutely brilliant and heartbreaking. But I

think you could help solve part of her problem. Because of your work with ritual, I think you could help her create some sort of 'marking' that could help her heal. Without her permission, I don't feel I should tell you exactly what she talked about, but if it's OK, I'd like to tell her about you and see if she'd meet with the two of us. The headlines are that her mom is a lesbian who broke up with her partner, so this girl's family has broken up, but no one is saying the word 'divorce.' I think you could help this kid, I really do."

The next week, Brynn called and said, "My student, Megan, does want to meet you. Would you come by the school some afternoon this week after 3:30 to talk with us?" We set a time.

When I found Brynn's classroom, she and a young woman with neon pink spiked hair were sitting in two of the student chairs, looking together at a photo-essay book. When I came through the door, Brynn smiled and waved me in, "Oh good, Monza, you found us—come on in!" She introduced Megan, who gave me the careful once-over.

I asked, "So how can I help?"

"Ms. Tillman told me about the rituals you do with people for all kinds of stuff. I'd like to have one with my sister, Dierdre. The deal is my mom and her mom have been partners for 20 years. And now they just broke up. But, see, when my mom birthed me, Connie adopted me, and when Connie birthed Dierdre, my mom adopted Dierdre. They were all into 'family forever' then, but now that they're not

together, when Connie moved out, she just took Dierdre—
her kid—and I stayed with Mom 'cause I'm really *her* kid.
They didn't even talk to us about it—we didn't even get one
of their famous 'sit down' talks, it just happened one night.
Each birth mom goes with her birth daughter. Done deal.
They hate each other right now, I get that. But they're just
totally 'mum'—clammed up—with us kids. Somehow they
seem to think that not talking bad about each other—not
talking at all—will make it all go away. My mom told me not
to talk to Connie 'cause they both agreed not to pull us kids
into the middle of their stuff. Her mom told Dee the same
thing. I tried calling her mom once, but she never returned
my call. So, screw her.

So the adoption seems just fake, you know? Family forever, right. It's really bogus. Dierdre and I have been together her whole life, and almost my whole life. I mean I was like
two when she was born, and we're sisters! Duh. I mean,
really. We've always been *told* we were sisters. We *are* sisters,
but our moms, just 'cause they're backing out on their deal,
are ripping us out of 'our deal.' They've divorced, although
they won't even say the word, but they've forced us kids to
'divorce' too. It's so frickin' lame. Dee and I are totally
wrecked. We see each other at school every lunch and hang
out and bawl and bitch about our moms, or sometimes we
just sit and stare at each other, like what the fuck just
happened to our lives? 'Scuse my language, but I'm really
upset."

"I'm not worried about your language, Megan! I appreciate you willing to be honest with me when we really don't know each other.   Please keep going."   Her teacher just smiled and nodded.

"OK, well, I've been pissed and sad and confused and … all over the place.   When Ms. Tillman gave us the 'family problems' assignment, I figured mine might just be unique."

"Maybe it is in your class, but it's pretty common in blended families. There *are* a lot of other kids who are suffering like you are.   And it makes me so sad, too, Megan.   You have every right to be as mad and sad and upset and confused as you are.   You really do.   And in my experience, almost all kids of divorce, whether their folks are gay or straight, suffer way more than would be necessary if adults would think more about the impact on their kids instead of being so caught up in their own pain and power struggles. Anyway, Megan, what feels right to you about creating some kind of ritual or ceremony with Dierdre?   What is it you'd most like to say and do?"

Megan stared out the window a couple of moments, and when she looked back at me and Brynn, she had tears in her eyes and didn't try to hide them.   "I want to tell her she really *IS* my sister!   And she always will be.   No matter who our mothers are or whatever they say or do.   I don't have any idea beyond that."

"That's absolutely enough!   It's clear, simple, and profoundly valid."

"But, like, how's that different than just—*talk!?*"

"Megan, I think that what makes a serious *talk* into a *ritual* is doing it in a place that is special to both of you, and combining the words you want to say with actually *doing* something, a meaningful action, and using or giving each other objects that make the words take on some kind of symbolic power that will last and even grow in its value to you—its significance—over time. Does that make sense?"

With her brightness shining, she replied, "Yeah, right, like in *Lord of the Rings* with the sword or the ring in the clearing, like that."

"Exactly. You and Dierdre can pick a spot that's special for you, and besides vowing to be sisters forever, you might give each other your promise written on a piece of paper or a gift (like a necklace or a charm bracelet), something you could each keep to remember what you say on that day. You could choose to have someone witness your promise, or you could choose to have your ceremony alone. You two can decide that together so it fits both of your needs. It doesn't have to be fancy ..."

"Yeah, like, we don't have to rent a hall, buy matching dresses and shoes, I get it. So, if Dee and I come up with a plan, can I run it by you?"

"Of course, here's my card." And I handed one over.

"What's about witnesses?"

"That's up to you. What would it mean to you to have them? Or what would it mean to do it alone? You and your sister can decide."

"Yeah, well, I'll run it by her, but I kinda like the idea of some adult, like a Good Parent, witnessing our 'contract', like. Especially since our moms are so not going to be there. They're not even talking to each other about us kids. They just send messages through us. I forgot to mention that we aren't supposed to talk to our other mom, but they can send messages through us. The lame-os. So, if we asked you, would you, like, watch us do this thing? Whatever it is we decide to do?"

"Yes, you can choose any adult you trust, and I'd be very willing to witness your ritual, offer a blessing for the two of you or be absolutely silent, whatever you wish. The value I find in having a witness is that you'll know there's a community always holding your commitment as serious, keeping the two of you in thought."

"Thanks. I get that."

As I got up to leave, I had one more thought. "Megan."

"Yes," she said.

"A letter can also be another form of ritual. Sometime, you and Dierdre might write a letter to your moms about how you feel, your own intentions, and what you'd like from them that they don't seem able to do right now. It might be a while before you felt ready, but I wanted to at least mention it as an option for the future."

Megan shrugged, said nothing. But I knew she wouldn't forget. This was a very sharp young woman, who Brynn said was being offered scholarships to several universities.

Megan called a week later. "Monza, Dee and I've decided how we want to do our Sisterhood Ritual. We have it all planned out, and we'd like for you and Ms. Tillman to be our witnesses. I talked to her about it after class today, and she said OK. Dee and I decided that you'd, like, 'hold the place' of our moms since they're not in a space where they can. And we'd like you to say some blessing words over us 'cause we can use all the help we can get. So when can we do it?"

The four of us met at a city garden on a weekend afternoon. Because of her trust of Megan, Dierdre was very open toward Brynn and me, talked naturally about her passion for bicycle racing and her race coming up the next day. The girls spread out a bedspread, and invited us to sit down. Megan took charge.

"We are sitting on one of the bedspreads we chose this past August for our room, when we imagined we'd be sharing a bedroom until I graduate. Now we live in two separate houses, but we both use our bedspread that matches the other's. Today we want to make it official: No matter what our moms do, ever, we are sisters forever. We have some words we've written together, and we want to say them to each other."

Then, one after another, each girl recited:

We are sisters.

We began our lives in a family, the family that Nell and Connie created. That family, which for all of our lives nurtured us, has changed. But even though Nell and Connie have divorced, and are not family anymore, we are still family. We are and will always be family to each other. We are sisters. Right now we live apart, with our own birth moms, but we know that won't always be true. Soon we'll be on our own. From the time we're on our own, able to make our own choices, I promise: wherever I am, for my whole life, you will always be welcome, you will always have a place. With this locket, I seal my promise: we are sisters, forever.

Each girl placed a locket around the other's neck. They reached out their arms to each other and hugged. Then they looked at me.

Looking into two young, serious faces, I said, "I want to offer my blessing on each of you, Megan and Dierdre, and both of you as always devoted sisters.

May you be sustained by your abiding love, your courage to claim what is true for you, and your creativity, which I believe will enable you to find ways to keep your sacred promise to each other for the rest of your lives, no matter what other challenges life may present." Looking at Brynn, then back at them, I added, "We will always hold you in our hearts, thanking your moms for making you sisters, and grateful that you know so well what you mean to each other that it no longer depends upon your moms to make it so. May your love grow deeper and more precious to each of you every year you live." I reached out, touching each of them lightly on the cheek. And then I sat back, letting the moment *be.*

After a comfortable amount of silence, Brynn reached out and hugged each girl, and then she asked if we could see their lockets. They proudly opened their beautiful gold lockets so we could both see: inside were current pictures of each of them. And I noticed that on the outside top of the locket, placed inside–an etched woven garland of leaves, were each girl's initials. "Buying 'em wiped out our savings," Megan said softly, "but we knew they were just the right thing. Thanks."

Not for the first or last time, I was moved by the wisdom of young ones. And I hoped there might come a day when the women who had given them life might come to the place where they could learn what their daughters had accomplished that day. That Nell and Connie could sometime celebrate that affirmation wholeheartedly. But I also knew that, whether or not such a time would ever come, their daughters had a bond that quite likely would *never* be broken.

Guidelines for a Ritual Created by Teenagers, the Next Generation Beyond Divorcing Parents

1. Make sure children/teenagers know they have the power to commit to stay bonded to their siblings even if the parents divorce.

2. Seek any assistance you might need from trusted adults to get the support you need for creating a ritual, while using your own creativity to make one that fits for you.

3. Once you've received the help you need, make a careful decision about whether you want to do the ritual just with your siblings, or have adult witness(es) present.

4. If the parents of a blended family are completely alienated, consider whether you and your siblings want to create a letter to send to the parents about wanting to maintain contact with both of them as well as each other.

    a. Both parents may care deeply for you, but each one might feel insecure about contacting the other parent's child(ren).

    b. If only one sibling feels that a ritual or letter is important, it is still worth doing. What is true for her/him should guide each ritual-maker.

Conclusion

*A*s you can see from the stories you've just read, there are as many options for rituals of divorce as there are people and situations. No way is *the right way*. What I have focused on here are stories that are both unique and also represent a wide range of common situations, offering guidelines I have gleaned from the people who've walked the path before you. From them, I have learned that certain choices, categories of attention, often provide the most hope of healing and sense of closure, which is why I've offered you a list of guidelines with each story as well as a planning guide at the end of this book.

Whether you are an individual wanting to heal the pain of divorce by yourself, for yourself, or whether you are hoping to mark this passage with an ex- or soon-to-be-ex-partner, with your friends, and/or with your children—whoever you are, whatever pain and loss, resolve and intentions still need your attention so that you can move forward in your life journey—my hope is that this book will be a useful tool for you.

If you are a professional who accompanies those traveling through the difficult territory of divorce, I believe you will find that each story here, though unique, also reinforces principles you can use to create rituals in situations that are similar in significant ways to the circumstances of your clients, parishioners, members, or participants.

Writing this book, and thus having the opportunity to think about the amazing variety of people I have met through this work, I am more grateful than ever to have undertaken this effort. My heart has grown through knowing them, sharing their yearnings to feel better and their bold resolve to make their lives different. Given the devastation most of them have felt at the time of their divorces, I have felt awe and deep respect for the courage they have found within—to take the necessary steps into unknown territory, to move forward, to reclaim their lives, to heal.

If you are reading this book because you are contemplating a divorce, are going through one now, or have already gotten one, but do not feel resolved, while I know you have to make your own choices about how to move forward through the difficulties and challenges, I do hope you trust, from reading these pages, that you are not alone. My best thoughts go with you.

Planning Guide

As you plan your own Divorce Ritual (or whatever name you choose to call it), you may find this planning guide useful. My hope is that it will clarify your thinking and give you a structure through which to put your feelings into words. Regard it as a map that can help you cover the main elements needed to accomplish the *gestalt* of a ritual's power to heal. Using it, you can create a ritual that meets your own unique needs.

If you want more ideas, you can review the guidelines at the end of the chapters. I have phrased the questions so that each person can answer them individually. While I know that in some cases two or more people—"we" instead of "I"—may plan a ritual, I think it is vital to have each person come to her/his own answers.

If you like, you can write out your answers to each of these questions, or you can just think about them.

The questions on the next page can help you create a ceremony that incorporates the four overarching components of ritual: *naming, honoring, attending to,* and *releasing.* These components are often woven throughout all the parts of a ritual.

Initial Questions:

Purpose: Why do I want to do a Divorce Ritual?

Function: What do I believe it will offer me or us?

Participants: Who do I want to share it with me or us? Why?

Place: Where do I want to have the ritual?

Is it a place where we can focus without distraction?

What is the significance of the place to me?

Why do I believe that space will contribute to the comfort, healing, and peacefulness I'm seeking?

Is it a place where everyone who is participating will be comfortable and feel safe?

Ritual Elements:

1. **What do I want to name as my need and/or desire for doing this ritual?**

   Do I want to create a process that will make my children feel secure?

   Do I want to shift from a negative focus to a positive one?

   Do I want to stop feeling helpless, or like a victim?

   Do I want to release bitterness?

   Do I want to reclaim my values and ethics?

   Do I want to reclaim my personal power?

   Do I want witnesses for support to gain strength?

   Do I want witnesses to listen and help hold me accountable?

   Do I want to let go of the past?

   Do I want to make commitments for the future?

   The list each person has for naming her/his need and desire for doing the ritual may have elements that are similar and others that are very different.

2. What do I want to affirm about the relationship that is ending or has ended?

Are there things I still value in that relationship? If so, what are they?

What am I glad to have learned or to have experienced in this relationship?

Are there things I've gained in my life from the relationship?

What hard lessons did I learn that I value?

What is/are the most important thing(s) I got out of this relationship?

3. What do I want to release, let go of?

What things do I regret doing or not doing in the relationship that is ending or has ended?

Are there things I regret saying or not saying?

Are there ways I regret not having taken better care of myself in the relationship?

Are there ways I regret not having taken better care of my children?

For what do I need to forgive myself in order to let go of guilt?

What do I need to let go of about my ex to free myself from feeling like a victim?

Are there any power struggles with my ex that I need to let go of?

What do I need to do to let go of any feelings of bitterness?

What, if any, litanies of wrongdoings do I repeat that I want to let go of?

Are there ways I badmouth my ex to myself or to my children that I want to let go of?

How can I help my children let go of pain surrounding this divorce? *(Discuss with children & teens if possible)*

What do my children need to let go of?
(Discuss with children & teens if possible)

4. What are my intentions as I move on after this divorce?

(I see release as having two parts: Clarifying and saying 1) what we don't need from the past, what keeps us entrenched, and 2) what hopes or prayers we want to release—as in sending forth our intentions—into the future)

What do I intend to change, reclaim, believe about myself?

Is there something I want to stop (habit, tendency, weakness, addiction)?

What do I want to never allow again in my life?

How can I move forward in greatest strength, with the most constructive power?

How do I want to deal with or speak to my ex, if we share a child or children?

What are my intentions for ensuring my children's greatest security, strength?

What are their intentions?
(Discuss with children & teens if possible—if they are participating in the ritual and even if they aren't)

5. **What actions or objects do I want included in the ritual to symbolize a commitment I am making?**

What do I want to do and/or what object do I want to give to myself to symbolize my promises to myself?

What do I want to do and/or what object do I want to give to my children to symbolize my promises to them?

What would I like to receive from the person or people who share in this ritual with me?

What would I like them to say? Do? Sing? Give to me so that I can remember their hopes for me?

Acknowledgments

As I complete this project, I am especially grateful for ...

All who have entrusted me with their stories of healing through divorce. I pray that I have done you justice in these pages, and that others will gain strength from your brave examples.

Emily Weaver, MFT, who first asked me for an excerpt of my chapter on divorce rituals as a resource for her participation in a conference panel. Emily, you inspired me to expand that chapter into this book. Thank you!

David Fink, J.D., for sage legal and technical advice.

Dear friends and colleagues near and far who support this non-traditional pastoral work I do.

My colleagues in the Redwood Writers, who inspire me to take my writing practice seriously, whatever project I undertake, and my stresses as a Writer much more lightly than I would without them.

My daughter, Ami Atkinson, and son-in-love, Jesse Combs, both of whom are children of divorce. I wish I could have made your childhoods easier, and I watch with awe and respect your commitment to making and sustaining family. You two—and, of course, our precious Sam and Will—are my treasures!

My sister, Debbie Dacus, for supporting me in countless ways during this past year—before and after our mother's death—for sharing the genesis of this work with me, and for cheering me on all the way.

Vicki Dello Joio, whose friendship and generosity bring increasingly precious gifts to my life, whose ear for dialogue is always 'spot on'! I love writing and editing a room away from you in our "Weaverville Writing Centre," nourished by safety, reciprocity, and great food!

Judith Cope, who gifts my work with skillful editing, grace under pressure, and—most of all—steady love for over 30 years.

Nancy Cleary, of Wyatt-MacKenzie Publishing—once again—for ushering this new book into the world. You are, truly, the best midwife a book could have, and the best ally an author could hope for.

And, as always, Sharon Strand Ellison, my partner in life, whose laser-mind and enormous heart make everything I am and do better.

About the Author

Dr. Monza Naff, of Oakland, CA, is a writer, teacher, consultant, speaker, and facilitator of workshops on writing and personal growth, team-building and leadership development, and creativity and spirituality in the workplace. A highly regarded design-er and leader of ritual, Monza has worked with groups of all sizes, galvanizing individuals into community wherever she goes.

For 26 years (1970-1996), Monza taught literature and writing in several colleges and universities-most recently on the faculty of the Robert D. Clark Honors College at the University of Oregon. Since 1996, she has been coaching writers, individual and corporate clients, and people desiring non-traditional rituals at times of transition.

Daughter of two ordained ministers, Monza was raised in a progressive Protestant background. She was originally licensed for ecumenical ministry in her family's denomination. Ordained, she is now a spiritual leader in the tradition of Unitarian-Universalism.

She is the author of an award-winning book of poetry, *Healing the Womanheart*, as well as *Exultation: A Poem Cycle in Celebration of the Seasons*, and *Must We Say We Did Not Love?: A Need for Divorce Rituals In Our Time*. In all of her work, Monza reveals a gift for helping people find the extraordinary in the ordinary.

Praise for
Naff's Other Works

About *Healing the Womanheart*

The kindest poetry a heart could imagine—this is indeed a book of healing.   *Ursula K. LeGuin*

A work of courage, challenge and joy.... In these poems Monza takes up the inconsolable sufferings of the world and transforms them into song.   *Mara Faulkner, OSB, PhD*

About *Exultation: A Poem Cycle In Celebration of the Seasons*

The poems of *Exultation* act as shofars to the soul, calling upon us to remember: to feel, sense, know in our very beings that we are connected through our cycles to all that is alive.... Read these words aloud. Chant, sing, intone them and experience a spirit that comforts and quiets, uplifts and inspires all at the same time. This quartet is a masterpiece.

Vicki Dello Joio, Qigong Master Teacher, Founder of Way of Joy, and Adjunct Faculty, JFK University

These poems of *Exultation* are the modern ode at its best and provide a deep well of reassurance for all who hope for healing.   *Glenn Routt, Professor Emeritus of Theology, Brite Divinity School*

You may contact Dr. Monza Naff at:
monzanaff@aol.com
phone: 510-655-8084, fax: 510-655-8082
or 4100-10 Redwood Rd., #316, Oakland, CA 94619

Printed in the United States
111783LV00001B/98/P